1000 Best Oz.

MW01614541

PREFACE
OVER A 1000 OF THE BEST JOKES AND STORIES EVER TOLD IN THE OZARKS

These stories were told around campfires, and pot-bellied stoves; on fishing trips, at a gathering of fox hunters, on the bench of the spit and whittle club, and about any occasion where Ozarkers would get together. Now they are heard at coffee shops, community gatherings, the sale barn, the barber shop, or even the hair dressers, but it is still the same style of Ozark humor that has lasted for over a century.

At gatherings, while telling stories, we are constantly urged to write them down so they can be handed down as our legacies here in the Ozarks. So here are a few of the better stories that I remember.

There are of course hundreds more that I have forgotten at this time, or ones that I did not see a value of including. You may have heard many of these, but if you are like me you will enjoy being refreshed with them.

I would like to document the origin or creator of each story or quote, but it is impossible to know or even to remember the source of every one of them. I have listed a few that I am real sure of.

Having this book on hand would especially be good for businessmen, salesman, speakers, emcees, at the coffee shop, or anyone meeting people. You can have a new story for each occasion. "Laughter is the jam on the toast of life. It adds flavor, keeps it from being too dry and makes it easier to swallow." (Diane Johnson.)

ACKNOWLEDGEMENT

To Frank L. Martin, III, West Plains, Mo. Quill, who has so diligently read, corrected and advised on the manuscript and to Ben Dennis, West Plains, Mo. for doing the art work.

1999 © Bob Hinds
P.O. Box 100
Willow Springs, MO 65793

5th Printing

ABOUT THE AUTHOR

I'm sure you will enjoy the humor of Bob Hinds. He is one of the country's most entertaining, motivating, and humorous after-dinner speakers. He has entertained and inspired audiences in most mid-western states as well as foreign countries.

It has been my privilege to attend many of his speaking engagements. At each event he was always proclaimed as the most outstanding speaker they ever had.

Laughter not only has a place in the business world, it is a necessity. It can be the edge that turns a mediocre program into a success story.

Bob has shared the stage with such greats as Jimmy Dean, deans of Colleges, U.S. Senators and Governors. For 30 years he has entertained crowds, from companies, conventions, to graduations and agriculture events, in many states as well as around the world.

Bob entertains audiences with how things look through the eyes of an Ozark Hillbilly Auctioneer. He was one of the leading purebred Auctioneers in the Midwest for a period of 15 years.

Bob Hinds was selected to be the first foreign judge of livestock shows in Japan. He has operated one of the nations foremost purebred livestock farms for 40 years.

Because of his success, his picture is hung in the University of Missouri Pavilion Honors Gallery.

Guy Carter, PHD, Superintendent of Schools , Independence, Mo.

WHAT JUST A FEW AUDIENCES HAVE SAID ABOUT BOB HINDS

Buffalo FFA – Best banquet speech we've ever had with strings of jokes and bits of advice that we will not forget.

University of Missouri Animal Husbandry Department – Your presentation of humor and advice came at a time of day when we surely needed a breath of fresh air.

Salem High School – Because of inducing the constant laughter along with stimulating our creative thinking, it was by far the best program we've had in my 13 years here.

Texas Tech College, Lubbock, Texas. – Your humorous and enlightening speech was just what our convention needed to get it started off in the right manner.

Independence, Mo. Lion's Club – Your humorous speech was the best we've had in our 50 years of existence.

Minneapolis, Minn. – Your speech was one that we have always been looking for to start our state conventions off with.

Humansville FFA – Your humorous and enlightening speech made our banquet a success. Your stimulating remarks gave us the encouragement and confidence to make ourselves better.

Our Annual Ohio State Conference was a great success due mainly to your concluding it with that very humorous and inspirational speech.

Frank L. Martin III, Publisher

ALPHA

1. I'm so old my insurance company only sent me a half a calendar.

2. I'm so old that to me the daily double is prune juice and an enema.

3. Man is not complete until he is married. Then he is finished.

4. "Do you ever wake up grumpy?" "No, I usually let her sleep."

5. Have I told you about my grandchildren?" "No, and I appreciate it."

6. I've used up all of my sick days, so I'm calling in dead.

7. The trouble with giving advice is that people want to repay you.

8. What's the difference in in-laws and out-laws? Out -laws are wanted.

9. She's so fat when she walks backward, she starts beeping

10. She's so ugly when she went to the plastic surgeon, he added a tail.

11. What do you call a cow that's just given birth? Decaffeinated.

12. Do you know what an Ozark credit card is? - A siphon hose.

13. Anatomy; Something everybody has, but which always looks better on a girl.

14. Trying to make ends meet here today is like being a pickpocket in nudist camp.

15. I went to the surgeon and asked him what he could do for me for $500. He said I can send you a get well card.

16. Do you know how to tell a rich Ozarkian from a poor one? The rich one has two cars jacked up in his front yard.

17. If you get there before I do, you make a blue mark. If I get there before you, I'll rub it out.

18. Plumber to lady client; "Maam, this is your bill, plus S50 for your husband helping me."

19. My wife is such a bad driver she got a ticket for driving up the side of a building. But she met another woman driver coming down.

20. What grade are you in son? "I'm in the 6th." "Is this the first time in the 6th ?"

21. Her husband getting out of bed said, "I've decided to get up and go to work after all. I'll call in sick some other day when I feel better."

22. My Bonnie looked into her gas tank, To see how much gas she could see; She lit a small match to assist her, Oh bring back my Bonnie to me.

23. Cow manure is good for chapped lips. It won't heal them, but you sure won't lick them.

24. Grandpa's just got one ear. He can still hear, but just catches every other word.

25. My wife and I had a big argument. I asked her how would she like it

if I didn't see her for about three days? She said that will be just fine. And I didn't see her the first day, I didn't see her the second day or the third day; on the fourth day I could see her just a little bit out of one eye.

26. BLONDE JOKE: When the blonde came home and found her husband in bed with another woman, she just picked up the gun and pointed it to her own head. Her husband said, "No, No, Don't do that!!" The blonde said, "Shut up. Your next."

27. They're changing all of the phone systems around now. The other night I made a call to Chicago, and when I finished, I ask the operator what the charges were. She said, "That will be five dollars sir." I said, "Five dollars? Why ma-am, down here in the Ozarks, we can call to hell and back for five dollars." She said, "Yes sir, but down there, that's a local call."

28. How did I actually find my wife? Well, a bunch of us Ozark country boys heard that someone was bringing a wagonload of girls to town from way back in the hills. When they got there with them, I just picked the ticks off of one of them and she followed me home.

29. An Ozarker was coon hunting and fell off of a steep cliff. As he was falling, he caught a limb with both hands. Pretty soon he hollered out, "Is anyone up there that can help me?" A loud voluminous voice came down, I CAN HELP YOU. Who are you? I AM THE LORD. What do you want me to do Lord. TURN LOOSE OF THAT LIMB. After a short hesitation, he called out, "Is there anyone else up there."

30. Patrolman writing ticket kept swatting flies. He said, "What kind of flies are those?" Passenger said, "Circle flies." "Why circle flies?" Because they only circle around "horses" butts." "Look fellow. Are you referring to me as a "horses rear?" "No, I'm not sir. But you sure can't fool those flies."

31. He told the boys at the coffee shop that next week is our 50th wedding anniversary. He told them that he took his wife to South America for their 25th anniversary. "Oh, my that was great. What are you going to do for the 50th one?" "I'm thinking about going back down there and picking her up."

32. My wife is on a diet and I've eaten so much green stuff that I have to tie a kerosene rag around each ankle to keep the cut worms from chewing my drawers off. (Pat Cash)

33. A little boy was told by his teacher, "You're going to have to stop speaking out in the classroom or I'll have to punish you." The little boy said, "I know, teacher, but I just can't help it. You see, my father was a preacher, and my mother is a woman."

6

34. A man and his young daughter were in an elevator with several people, including a gorgeous blonde. Just as the elevator door opened, the blonde slapped the man in the face and left in a huff "I don't like her either," the little girl said to her stunned father. "When she stepped on my foot, I pinched her!!"

35. I will pay my delinquent bill as soon as I get my mother paid off. A note came back: Dear Sir: After checking our records, we have concluded that we have done more for you than your mother ever did; we've carried you for fifteen months.

36. Tenderfoot; "How can I tell mushrooms from toadstools? Second Class Scout: "Eat some before you go to bed. If you wake up the next morning, they're mushrooms."

37. An Ozarker got a job in an airport and a customer asked him why that mistletoe was hanging over the luggage rack? He said, "So you can kiss your luggage "good-bye."

38. The judge had just passed sentence when he heard the accused muttering vigorously. "What's that?" demanded the judge. "it sounded like cussing." Nossir, not on your life," said the defendant. "All I said was 'God am the judge, God am the judge'."

39. A kid was swimming in the pond. His dad said, "I told you not to swim in the pond." "I fell in." "If you fell in, how come your clothes are dry?" "I took them off, I had a hunch I might fall in."

40. "You have two sisters?" "yes" "What's their names?" "Hortense and Lassie." "Well, Lassie is a dog." "Wait 'til you see Hortense."

41. "You say that you're name is Chow mein and you were a Japanese kamikaze pilot in World War II? How could that be? You would have gone on a suicide mission and be dead? "My name is Chicken Chow Mein."

42. A man was touring a nut house and noticed a man in the nut house hollering "Lu-Lu, Lu-Lu" on and on. What's wrong with him? He was engaged to Lu-Lu and she dropped him. On the next floor a man was hollering "Lu-Lu, Lu-Lu" on and on. What's wrong with him? He married Lu-Lu.

43. Three couples approached the Pearly Gates and asked permission from Saint Peter to enter. To the first husband he responded, "You may not enter heaven. All of your life you've been obsessed with money. Why, you even married a woman named Penny!"

He then turned to the second husband and responded, "You may not enter heaven. All of your life you've been obsessed with food. Why, you even married a woman named Candy."

Taking his wife gently by the hand and looking very sad, the third husband said, "Come on, Fanny, we might as well get out of here!" (Minnie Pearl)

44. The Blonde got hail damage on her car so she took it to the body shop. The man said he could fix it, but you can do it yourself. Just take it home and blow on the tail pipe. While blowing on the tail pipe, her blonde neighbor asked what she was doing. She told her she was blowing on the tail pipe to pop the hail dents out. The second blonde said, "Well silly, don't you know you have to roll the windows up first."

ACCIDENT

1. After a car wreck, the driver came rushing back to the other and said, "What's the matter? Are you blind." "Blind? I hit you, didn't I?"

2. After a car accident, the patrol asked the driver how this accident happened. The man said, "My wife fell asleep in the back seat."

✓ 3. How bad are you hurt? I don't know. I haven't seen my lawyer yet.

4. Most accidents happen within 25 miles from home. That's why the Pollack moved.

5. The reason there were fewer wrecks in the horse and buggy days was because the driver didn't depend wholly on his own intelligence.

6. It's so cold here that if you had an accident, you'd have to wait 'til Spring to see if you're going to bleed. (Bob Hope.)

✓7. I lost my watch. I dropped it in the sheep dip – it took all of the ticks out of it.

8. After a fall to the sidewalk from the third floor, a passerby asked him what happened. He said, "Don't know. I just got here myself."

9. Two Ozark buddies applied for a truck driving job. Had to work together as a pair. Couldn't be separated. One question on the interview was, what would you do if you were going down a long steep hill and saw the road blocked at the bottom of the hill, and your brakes went out when you stepped on them. "I'd wake up my buddy Leroy." "Why that?" "Because Leroy ain't never seen no bad accident."

10. It is reported that during the big power "blackout" in the east, many persons were trapped in elevators between floors in the office buildings in New York City. Police and firemen emergency crews did yeoman work in rescuing those unfortunates, concentrating their efforts to aid the sick or disabled. In the course of operations a rescue squad attempted to reach the trapped occupants of one elevator and, to find if this were an emergency, shouted up the elevator shaft, "Are there any pregnant women in there?" The answer came back quickly from some unidentified gentleman, "No, we're hardly even acquainted yet."

ANIMALS

Dogs

1. When I was young, my parents got a dog. I was jealous of the dog. So they got rid of me.

2. Guest at yard gate looking at a potentially mean dog: The host said, "Come on in." "Will the dog bite?" "Don't know. That's what we want to find out."

3. A ferocious dog comes toward a young couple. The boy runs. The girl said, I thought you said you would face death for me. "Yes. But that darn dog isn't dead."

4. Why is that dog setting there looking at me all of the time? "Suppose it's because you have the plate he usually eats out of?"

5. If dogs could talk, it would take a lot of fun out of owning one.

6. You could just ask my stock dog for any size animal that you wanted and he would bring it in to you. But some Japanese were over here the other day and they asked for it in the metric system, and now it's got him all fouled up.

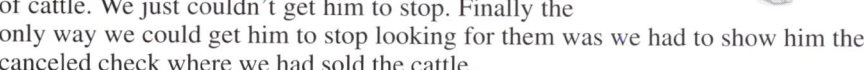

7. We had 100 head of cattle across the road and it was "Old Shep's" job to bring them up around the feeders every morning. He did a wonderful job of it too. But we sold the cattle and it really disappointed the dog. Every morning he would jump the fence, cross the creek run, search the brush patches looking for that herd of cattle. We just couldn't get him to stop. Finally the only way we could get him to stop looking for them was we had to show him the canceled check where we had sold the cattle.

8. I only tell this story when my wife is not around. Every man is entitled to one good dog and one good woman in a lifetime, and I've had my good dog.

9. A policeman stopped me with my dog setting in the car beside me. He said, "Does the dog have a license?" I said, "No. He doesn't need one. I do most of the driving."

10. A man noticed my dog setting by me in the theater. He was enthralled at the dog's interest in the picture. When there was something sad, the dog would cry, and when there was something amusing, the dog would yip with glee. Finally, the man taped me on the shoulder, and said, "I'm amazed that the dog's so interested in the movie!" I replied, "Yes, this surprises me too. He didn't care a thing about the book."

11. The small boy cried bitterly when a big dog ran up and licked his face. "Did he bite you?" asked the anxious mother. "No," sobbed the little fellow, "but he tasted me."

12. There was a fellow waiting for a haircut. As he studied a big German Shepherd dog in the barber shop he was impressed by the way the dog intently watched every move of the barber. Finally he said to the barber: "It's amazing how interested that dog is in every move of your scissors. He must enjoy watching you work." "Well," said the barber, "it isn't exactly that. But every now and then I

accidentally snip off a piece of ear – he really goes for that!"

13. Lately my wife has insisted on getting a Chihuahua. These dogs are the ugliest thing alive; bleary, buggy-eyed things. They look like a mouse on steroids.

14. I wanted to call him Spot, but there is not enough dog, so we called him Speck.

15. It's not easy to play with a dog that you can kill with a Frisbee.

16. He loves to ride in the car, but he is too small to look out, so we just describe the landscape to him..

17. I finally put suction cups on his feet so he can stick on to the windows and look out. He just loves them. He does get a little nervous, though, when I roll the windows up and down.

18. He likes it a lot better, though, since I started riding him inside.

19. He especially likes it when I take him to the drive-in bank and the teller lets him ride up and down the little tubes.

20. One lady in the next car over said, "Did he leave a deposit?" (Jim Stafford.)

21. Henry's dad paid the tuition, bought the books, and paid the room and board for college, but didn't give him any spending money. All of his friends had spending money, so Henry devised a scheme to get some extra money. When he was home for Thanksgiving, he told his dad they had a class up there that could teach Old Shep, Dad's beloved dog, to read for $250. He thought so much of Old Shep that he sure wanted him to be able to read, so he sent him back with Henry, along with the $250. Later, Henry wrote home and said that Old Shep was reading legal documents, and that they could teach him to talk for $500. Dad sure wanted Old Shep to talk, so he sent the $500. Later, Henry wrote his dad and said that Old Shep was setting there quoting the formulas out of a Chemistry Lab book. Henry also said that they could teach him to smoke for $1,000, of which his dad also promptly sent. His dad could hardly wait for Old Shep to come home for Christmas and see all of these great tricks. He met them at the train station, but there was no Old Shep. His dad, being really disappointed, said, "Where's Old Shep?" "Well, dad, it's like this. We were coming along and Old Shep was setting beside me, smoking a cigar and reading the Wall Street Journal. Then suddenly he looked outside the train window and said, "Isn't that Aunt Minnie's house where your dad used to come and see her all of the time?" I didn't like that a bit so I just threw him out the window." "You did the right thing, son. There's nothing worse than a blabber mouth dog." (Paul Belts,)

22. Dachshunds are not recommended as pets in Alaska. They keep the door open too long, going in and out of the house.

23. Looks like a smart dog you've got there," remarked a friend. "Smart! All I have to say is, 'Are you coming or aren't you?' And he either comes or he doesn't."

24. The neighborhood kids were in the front lawn when a fire truck zoomed past with the station mascot sitting on the front seat. The children began discussing the dog's duties in connection with the truck. "They use him to keep the crowd back at a fire," said a five-year-old girl. "No," said another, "they carry him for good luck." A six-year-old boy brought the argument to an abrupt halt. "They use the dog," he announced firmly, "to find the fire plug."

25. The Ozarker was trying to get back away from a very mean dog that was just

a growling and a hissing at him. A parrot was in a cage behind him and kept saying, 'Hello, hello, hello.' Finally he'd had enough of the parrot and turned around and said, "Parrot, don't you know anything except hello?" And the parrot said, "Sic 'em."

26. A man walked into his back yard one morning and found a gorilla in a tree. He called a gorilla-removal service, and soon a serviceman arrived with a stick, a Chihuahua, a pair of handcuffs and a shotgun. "Now listen carefully," he told the home owner. "I'm going to climb the tree and poke the gorilla with this stick until he falls to the ground. The trained Chihuahua will then go right for his, uh, sensitive area, and when the gorilla instinctively crosses his hands in front to protect himself, you slap on the handouffs." "Got it," the home owner replied. "But what's the shotgun for?" "If I fall out of the tree before the gorilla," the man said, "shoot the Chihuahua." (Paul Belts.)

Livestock

1. An old lady met a little girl leading a big cow. "You're mighty small to be doing that. Where are you going?" "To the bull ma-am," was the reply. Shocked, the lady said, "Can't your father do that?" Very politely, the little girl said, "Oh no, Ma-am, it has to be a bull."

2. A cattleman was moving a prize bull and the bull laid down in the middle of the road. He couldn't get him up by kicking, clubbing, or switching, and he was causing a road block. A good looking lady got out of a car and said, "I'm an animal rights activist, and you can't beat dumb animals like that. Will you let me try?" She bent over the bull a moment and the bull immediately got up and run real fast down the road. The cattleman thanked her and said, "Ma'am, would you please tell me what you did to get that bull to move?" "I just tickled him in a certain place." "Well lady, would you mind tickling me in that same place, because I've got to catch that bull?"

3. Racehorse owner E. R. Bradley had all his horses' names begin with the letter B, including one called Bad News. When someone asked why he gave the horse a name with such a negative connotation, Bradley explained, "Bad News travels fast." (Jake Vinci.)

4. Three little pigs went into a bar. The first little pig went to the bathroom. Then the second little pig went to the bathroom. The third little pig just went up to the bar. The bartender asked the third little pig why he didn't go to the bathroom. He said, "I'm the little pig that goes 'Wee, Wee, Wee, all of the way home."

Snakes

1. Got bit on the back of my arm by a poisonous snake. "What did you do?" Cut a cross with my sharp knife and had a friend suck the poison out. A while back I was sitting on a log and got bit on the rear end." "My, what do you do then?" "You sure find out who your friends are."

Other Animals

1. A city slicker visiting an Ozark Mink Farm: "How many pelts per animal do you get?" The Ozarker replied, "You know, we've found that if we skin 'em more than once, it seems to make them pretty nervous."

2. As to Reagan's cautious support of Gorbachev: "Do not insult the mother alligator until after you have crossed the river."

3. Compare the present situation to that of the mouse who said, "Don't give me any more of your free cheese. Just get my head out of this trap."

4. What should you do when you see an endangered animal that is eating an endangered plant?

5. The little Ozark boy told his dad that he saw a miracle today. His dad asked him about it. The boy said, "Mommy went out to dump the trash this morning and a mouse run up her dress, and she caught it with her knees." "Why, that's no miracle, son," his dad replied. The boy said, "Well, dad that wasn't the miracle. The miracle was that mommy squeezed that little ole mouse so hard she squeezed a gallon of water out of him."

ARMY

1. Tell your friends to come with you. I have no friends. I'm the bugler.

2. Mess Sergeant: "Look here, wise guy, I was fixing chow long before you were even born. Rookie: "All right. But why serve it now?"

3. ARMY – In Bosnia: "Of course you fellas know why I'm here. I forgot to take the Bush sticker off my car."

4. He wanted to join the army, but didn't like to march. A buddy told him that paratroopers don't march. They just jump and a truck picks you up and takes you back to camp. On his first jump, he pulled the cord and nothing happened. Pulled the second cord and nothing happened. As he was approaching the ground, he said, "With this kind of luck, I'll bet that darn truck won't be there either."

5. An Irish soldier on duty in Egypt during World War II received a letter from his wife saying there wasn't an able-bodied man left and she was going to have to dig the garden herself. Pat wrote at the beginning of his next letter: "Bridget, please don't dig the garden; that's where the guns are." The letter was duly censored, and in a short time a lorryload of men in khaki arrived at Pat's house and dug up the garden from end to end. Bridget wrote to Pat in desperation, saying that she didn't know what to do, as the soldiers had got the garden dug up, every bit of it. Pat's reply was short and to the point: "Put in the spuds."

6. If a stealth bomber crashes in the forest, will it make a sound?

7. After a grueling day of training, which had included a ten-mile hike and completion of a difficult obstacle course, my son Eric's platoon of raw recruits quickly fell into bed. As Eric lay in the dark, he heard a voice recite a prayer: "Now I lay me down to sleep, I Pray the Lord my soul to keep, if I should die before I wake, thank you, Lord." There was a brief pause and then several voices said in

unison, "Amen."

8. After enlisting in the 82nd Airborne Division, I eagerly asked my recruiter what I could expect from jump school. "Well," he replied, "it's three weeks long." "What else?" I inquired. The first week they separate the men from the boys," he said. "The second week they separate the men from the fools." "and the third week?" I asked. "The third week the fools jump." (Tod Rejholec.)

9. A soldier was being chased by the MP's who wanted to send him to the Korean War. He saw a nun standing on the street corner in full regalia. He asked the nun if he could hide under her skirts. The nun said O.K. After the MP's had gone, he came out and said nun you have a nice set of legs for a nun. The nun said, Son, you didn't look far enough, I don't want to go to Korea either. (Darrell Peters.)

10. An Ozark boy went to the Gulf War and they had a colonel that was known as Fat Arsed Johnson. They didn't openly call him that though. One day he was the only one there as the phone rang in the motor pool. A sign there says, "Recruits Do Not Answer The Phone." It kept ringing and being a good old Ozark boy, he just answered it anyway. The giant voice came through, "Soldier, what vehicles do you have available over there? The Soldier looked around and replied, "Six Trucks, an Armored Tank, a half track, and Colonel Fat Arsed Johnson's command car. The Colonel said, "Soldier, do you know who you're talking to?" "No." "This is Col. Johnson." "Oh," There was a moment of silence. "Colonel, do you have any idea who you're talking to?" "No." The soldier said, "Bye, Bye, Fat Arsed!!"

AUTOMOBILE

1. I bought my wife a new car. She called me and said there was water in the carburetor. I said where's the car? She said in the lake. (Henny Youngman.)

2. My wife is such a bad driver she had three tickets on her written test.

3. Women not only drive as well as men, but they can do it on either side of the road.

4. Definition of a reckless driver: A man who lets his wife take the wheel.

5. Two women who were maneuvering their car into a tight parking space gave up after a valiant struggle when the driver shut off the motor and said to her companion: "This is close enough. We can walk to the curb from here."

6. Lady motorist: "Can you fix this fender so my husband won't know that I dented it?" Mechanic: "No, ma'am, but I can fix it so in about a week you can ask him how he did it."

7. Sign in an auto repair shop, "He who looketh upon a woman looseth a fender."

8. No driver needs manners who has a horn and a ten-ton truck. (Prochnow.)

9. Every year thousands die from gas. Some inhaled it, a few lit it, but most of them just stepped on it.

10. The speed and power of the new cars helps to bring places closer together. Like this world and the next.

11. A woman motorist jumped out of her car and shouted at the driver, "Why don't you people ever watch where you're driving? You're the fourth car I've hit this morning!"

12. A woman motorist was driving along a country road when she noticed a couple of repair men climbing telephone poles. "Fools!," she exclaimed to her companion, "They must think I never drove a car before."

13. A used car isn't what it's jacked up to be.

14. How do you double the value of a Yugo? Fill it up with gas.

15. I told the guy at the auto parts store I wanted a windshield wiper for my Yugo. He said, that sounds like a fair exchange.

16. I got a "Yugo" car. You go buy a car this week, and you go buy another next week.

17. A man run out of gas and walked to a filling station to get gas and could only find a bed pan to get gas in. As he was pouring it in the tank, an Ozarker came along. After watching him a minute, he said, "I didn't know that would work. I've been paying $1.25 a gallon for it."

18. Let's drive over on Glenstone Street for awhile and watch the accidents.

19. A couple went to an auto dealer to look at compact cars. Told the price, the husband said: "But that's almost as much as the price of a big car!" "Yes," explained the enthusiastic dealer, "but if you want economy, you have to pay for it!"

20. The motorist saw the service station sign: "Last chance for 29-cent gas. State line one mile." He stopped, had his tank filled, then asked: "How much is gas across the line?" Replied the attendant: "Twenty-two cents."

21. Policeman: "Why didn't you stop when I yelled at you back there?" Lady Driver: "Oh, were you the one who yelled? I thought it was someone I had run over."

22. A plump, worried-looking little lady pulled into a service station. "My hands are so dirty they're about to pop," she exclaimed as she dashed to the ladies room.

23. The Ozarker came back from Hawaii and told his friends that January is sure the time to go over there. He said that no tourists are there then. He said that he was over there for ten days and he never saw a single out of state license plate.

24. A woman driver stalled her car at a traffic light. She tried desperately to start the engine, while behind her an impatient man rudely honked his horn. Finally, she got out and walked back. "I'm sorry," she said to the man, "but I can't start my car. If you'll go there and start it for me, I'll stay here and honk your horn for you."

25. Leaving the railroad station, the visitor herded his children onto the sidewalk and called to the cab driver, "How much to take the whole family to the zoo?" The cab driver, recognizing a bargain hunter, replied: "It'll be three dollars each for you and your wife. The four kids can all ride free." "That's mighty nice of you," the visitor said. Turning to the children he ordered: "Pile in, kids. Your ma and I will go by subway."

26. A man was stopped by the police and he quickly fastened his seat belt. The policeman asked him if he was driving with his seat belt fastened. The man said, "Yes." The police said, "Do you always fasten it through the steering wheel?"

27. Why do they lock gas station bathrooms? Are they afraid someone will clean them?

28. Talking cars are not always so good. I told a cop that I wasn't speeding, and the car said, "He was so." (Bob Hope.)

Bus

1. The height of hillbilly sophistication is illustrated by the hillbilly who sat next to the little old lady in the bus. He scratched himself leisurely, pulled off his shoes and two-week old socks, wiped his nose across the back of his hand and calmly asked, "Mam, do you mind if I smoke?"

2. Not a man on the crowded bus rose and gave the old lady a seat. One man was more thoughtful though. He tugged at her skirt and whispered, "Be on your toes at Market Street, lady. That's where I get off."

BIRDS

1. You'll soon see that there are more song birds in the Ozarks than jail birds.

2. Why did the chicken cross the road? To prove to the 'possum that it could be done.

3. I went to gather the eggs and I found a quarter. The next day I found 15 cents. On the third day, I found a dime. "What's going on?" "Don't know, unless my Old Hen's going through the change."

CHURCH

1. In Heaven there were four men chained to their chairs. Why? They're determined to return to the Ozarks.

2. Two brothers were in the bulk feed business together, and one of them joined the church. The preacher asked the other to join. He replied, "Preacher, if I join too, who will do the weighing?"

3. Preacher to farmer, who was haying on Sunday: "Don't you know God made the world in 6 days and rested on the 7th?" The farmer said, "Yes, I know, but He got done and I didn't."

4. "I'm going to baptize you and wash away all of your sins." "In that little Pool?"

5. An Ozarker was being baptized on a cold January day and they even had to break the ice in the river. When he came up out of the water, his friends on the bank hollered out, "Is the water cold, Uncle John?" "Naw, he replied." One friend said, "'Dip him again, preacher, he's still lying."

6. An Ozarker went in to a confession booth and the priest opened up the little window and said, can I help you sir? "You sure can. Is there any paper on that side?"

7. Walking down the street, two Ozarkers met a Catholic nun whose arm was in

a sling. "What's wrong with your arm, Sister?" asked one Hillbilly. "It's broken in three places," the Sister replied. "How did that happen?" asked the second Hill-billy. "I slipped in the bathtub," answered the Sister. After leaving, the first hillbilly asked the other, "What's a bathtub?" "Heck, I don't know," said his friend, "I'm not Catholic."

8. A man stood at the gates of Heaven when St. Peter stopped him and said, "Oh, no. You don't get into Heaven anymore just for being good. You have to have done something truly great. Have you done anything that you can say is really and truly great in your life?" The man thought for a minute and said, "I saw a group of Hell's Angels harassing an old lady so I kicked over the leader's bike, slapped him and spit in his face." "That's great," St. Peter said. "When did you do that?" "About three minutes ago," he replied.

****SLIP UPS****

9. Tonight's sermon: "What is Hell? Come early and listen to our choir prac-tice."

10. Don't let worry kill you. Let our church help.

11. There will be a potluck supper. Prayer and medication will follow.

12. For those of you who have children and don't know it, we have a nursery downstairs.

13. This being Easter Sunday, we will ask Mrs. Johnson to come forward and lay an egg on the alter.

14. Tuesday at 4 p.m. there will be an ice cream social. All ladies giving milk, come early.

15. Thursday at 5 p.m. there will be a meeting of the little mothers club. All ladies wishing to be little mothers, please meet with the pastor in his study.

16. The ladies of the church have cast off clothing of every kind, and they may be seen in the church basement on Friday afternoon.

17. A bean supper will be held on Saturday evening in the church basement. Music will follow.

18. Remember in prayer the many who are sick of our church and community.

19. On Sunday a special collection will be taken to defray the expenses of the new carpet. All those wishing to do something on the carpet, please come forward and get a piece of paper.

20. The service will close with little drops of water. One of the ladies in the choir will start quietly and the rest will join in.

****

21. Baptists; they're just like Tom Cats; always messing around, but you can't catch them at it.

22. A man was shouting "Amen!" in a Methodist Church. One of the Deacons came over and told him he'd have to be quiet. Said the man, "But I've got religion." The Deacon replied, "Well, shut up you didn't' get it in this church."

23. A Mormon was milking a cow and she stuck her foot in the bucket. Then she switched him in the face with her dirty tail, and as a good Mormon he still didn't do anything. Then the cow kicked him out in the manure. He then picked up a 2x 4 and drew back and said, "I'm a good Mormon and I can't hit you, but I'll sell you to a Presbyterian who will beat the devil out of you."

24. I passed a store the other day. There were some fish outside and they smelled pretty bad. I asked the storekeeper what kind of fish they were.

Said he – "They're Baptist fish"

Said I – "Why do you call them Baptist fish?"

Said he – "Because they spoil so quickly after being taken out of the batter!"

25. Many a man is the pillar of the church – an outside pillar.

26. It's harder to get men to church than women, probably because men aren't interested in what other men are wearing.

27. A man down on his luck asked God, "How long is a million years to you?" "Oh, it's just like a second to me." "How much is a million dollars to you?" "Oh, it's just like a penny to me!" "Well, God will you give me a million dollars?" God said, "Wait a second." (Rick Wheeler`)

28. MONEY - There's no reason to be the richest man in the cemetery. You can't do any business from there.

29. "What are sins of omission?" The Sunday School class was asked. One lad volunteered, "They're sins we should have committed – and didn't."

30. Two men died and went to Heaven and one asked how the other died. "I thought my wife was running around on me and I looked all over the house and had a heart attack." "Man, why didn't you look in the refrigerator, and we would both still be there."

31. Do any of you out there in the congregation believe in reincarnation? One person raised his hand. "Hello, there. It's good to see you again."

32. They threw the liquor in the river, then the choir begin singing, "Shall We Gather At The River."

33. Let's do something religious. Get up and start calling off Bingo.

34. If all the people who sleep in church were placed end to end, they would be more comfortable.

35. The 98-year-old man said, "As old as I am, I have more friends in Heaven than down here. If I don't die pretty soon, they'll think I didn't make it." (Rick Wheeler.)

36. I don't understand why religion and science can't get along with each other. What's wrong with counting our blessings with a computer?

37. SAD – We sing "Make a Joyful Noise Unto the Lord" while our faces reflect the sadness of one who just buried a rich aunt that left everything to her pregnant hamster. (Erma Bombeck.)

38. "A man sent me a card and said that he would kill me if I didn't stay away from his wife." "Are you going to?" "How can I? He didn't sign it."

39. The reverend Jimmy Baker said that Christ died for our sins. Dare we make his martyrdom meaningless by not committing them.

40. The sinning is the best part of repentance.

41. Ingersol, an atheist, asked a little girl who was on her way to Sunday School, if she believed all of that stuff that they were telling her. She said, "I certainly do." "Do you actually believe Jonah was swallowed by a fish?" "Yes." "Well, what did he eat and drink for three days?" "I don't know, but I'll ask him when I get to heaven." "What if he isn't there?" "Then you ask him."

42. When a 10-year-old was asked what he learned in Sunday School, he said,

"We learned that Gos sent Moses behind enemy lines to rescue the Israelites from the Egyptians. Moses called for engineers to build a pontoon bridge over the Red Sea. After crossing it, they saw the Egyptians tanks coming. Moses radioed headquarters to send bombers to blow up the bridge and save the Israelites." "Is that really the way your teacher told that story?" "Well, not exactly, but if I told it her way, you'd never believe it."

43. An old lady attended a revival meeting and the preacher talked on faith. He said that faith could move mountains. This is just what this lady was wanting to hear, because she always wanted that mountain moved that was on the east side of her house. So she prayed all night that God would move that mountain. The next morning she just could hardly wait until daylight. When she did look out, she said, "Just as I thought. The mountain's still there."

44. A preacher who was filling in for the regular one used this example: Do you see that broken window pane over there with the cardboard in it? It's not the real pane. It's a substitute, like I am a substitute for the real preacher. After a long sermon, he was shaking hands with people as they came out. One old man walking with a cane shook hands with him and said, "Preacher, you're sure no substitute, you're a real pane."

45. "Is that the big fat hog there?" "Sir, that isn't any way to address the head of our church. That's disrespectful" "OK, I just wanted to donate a million dollars to your church." "Sir, that's OK. I think I see the Big Fat Pig coming now."

46. Boudreax was a good little Southern boy who was always a good Bible scholar. He died and went to Heaven. St. Peter said that he would have to answer one question before entering. "OK, what is it?" "What is God's first name?" "That's easy. It's Howard." "How do you get that?" "Howard Be Thy Name."

47. After his daddy had just so kindly fixed his tricycle, the little boy asked his mother, "Is daddy as smart as God?" The mother replied, "No, not quite, but he's as smart as God was when God was at your daddy's age.

48. "Your daddy gets up so early that he sees God go to work."

49. "I'm sorry about Uncle Jim." (crying). "Why are you crying, he's been dead for 5 years?" "Yes, but he owed me $5 and he's up in Heaven now. Well, I think I'll just go up there and meet him and get it and then come right back!" "What if he isn't up there?" "Then will you get it?"

50. Asked to buy a ticket to a church benefit, a man said, "Sorry Reverend, I won't be able to attend. But my spirit will be with you. "Good," said the preacher. "I have $0.50, $1.00, and $2.00 tickets. Where would you like your spirit to sit?"

51. Swiped this Story from Sports Afield: Two backsliders, fishing on Sunday morning, felt pretty bad about it. One said to the other, "It's Sunday. I ought to be in church." To this the other angler replied, "I couldn't go to church even if I were home. My wife's sick."

52. Every evening I pour my worries over to God. He's going to be up all night anyway. (Mary C. Crowley.)

53. One Sunday my teenage son was in church. When the collection plate was passed around, he pulled a dollar bill from his pocket and dropped it in. Just at that moment the person behind him tapped him on the shoulder and handed him a $20 bill. Secretly admiring the man's generosity, my son placed the $20 in the plate

and passed it on. Then he felt another tap from behind and heard a whisper: "Son, that was your $20. It fell out of your pocket." (Mary Lowe.)

54. There are ending degrees of poverty, as indicated by this anecdote in the Lamar Daily Democrat: "The minister arose to address his congregation. 'There is a certain man among us today who is flirting with another man's wife. Unless he puts five dollars in the collection box, his name will be read from the pulpit.' When the collection plate came in, there were 19 five-dollar bills, and a two-dollar one with this note attached: 'Other three payday.'"

CHRISTMAS

1. Christmas: The time of year when Santa comes down the chimney and your savings go down the drain.

2. I have just finished my Christmas shopping – for last year.

3. If you really want to have an exciting Christmas, make an agreement with your wife not to exchange Christmas gifts. Then don't.

4. I was going to get my old hound a present, but all he wanted was a tree.

5. Smart kids today don't write Santa. They write Grandma.

6. I asked my 3-year-old grandson if he saw Santa last night. He said, "I didn't actually see him, but I heard what he said when he stumbled over my tricycle."

7. An Ozarker was with a group singing Christmas Carols. "Leon, Leon," he sang. The man next to him nudged him and whispered, "Stupid, turn your book over ... it's 'Noel, Noel.'"

8. Ma: "Pa, I don't think the neighbors like the new drum we got Johnny for Christmas." Pa: "Why not?" Ma: "They gave him a knife and asked him if he knew what was in the drum."

9. With hemlines at their present height, I don't think Santa Claus is even gentleman enough to look a lady in the eye.

10. The Supreme Court ruled that Washington, D.C. can't have a Nativity scene this year. It wasn't for economic reasons; they just couldn't find three wise men and a virgin.

11. "I'm doing away with Santa this year. Why have Santa only one day each year when you can have Bill Clinton every day?"

12. Shopping for Christmas became too difficult for my wife, so she decided to just send checks. On each card she wrote, "Buy your own present," then mailed the letters. After Christmas, under a stack of papers she found the gift checks she had forgotten to include in the letters.

13. "Yes-siree, I always shake a package. If it don't gargle, I don't open it."

14. Bob Hope said it was so crowded shopping that a lady was in the sleepwear department trying on a night gown when she asked the clerk, "It's my size. Why is it so tight?" Bob Hope said, "Because I'm in here with you."

15. Dynasty is planning a special kind of Christmas show. The big moment comes when Joan Collins is trying to get Santa Claus to stay over-night. It's the 1st time Santa sent the reindeer on ahead. (Bob Hope.)

16. They're giving talking gifts this Christmas. This is the first time you can return the gift and the gift can explain why.

17. One talking camera tells you when you shouldn't be taking that kind of a picture.

18. There was a salesman from New York traveling down in the Ozarks during Christmas Season. He drove into the small hill town and noticed a beautiful Nativity scene on the lawn of the church. He was puzzled tho' because the Wise Men all wore firemen's helmets. He stopped in the local cafe to have lunch. As he was chatting with the Ozark waitress, he remarked, "You certainly have a nice Nativity scene but I don't understand why the Wise Men are wearing fireman helmets?" She looked at him as if he had lost his mind. "You sure 'nuff are from up nath? Don't you ever read your Bible?" He said, of course he reads the Bible, every day. "Well," she said, "You don't remember what you read 'cause it very plainly says right here," as she showed him her Bible, "That the Wise Men came from afar." (Kenna Cameron.)

CLOCKS

1. A man was walking down the street with a grandfather clock on his back, going to get it repaired, and ran in to an old lady. She said, "Sonny Boy, why don't you carry a wrist watch like most people do?"

2. A workman was perched on top of a ladder, cleaning the clock above the entrance to a bank. An inquisitive patron hailed him, "Something wrong with the clock, mister?" "No," replied the workman, "I'm nearsighted."

CROSSBREDS

1. We're crossing Homing Pigeons with Wood Peckers so that when they get home, they can knock on the door.

2. We're crossing minks with kangaroos, so we can raise fur coats with pockets.

DEAF

1. "Uncle John, I'd like to borrow your wagon." "Heh." "Uncle John I'd like to borrow your wagon." "Heh." Can't hear you. If I could hear you. I wouldn't loan you my wagon."

2. Uncle Fred just has one ear. – Catches every other word though.

3. And this next speaker is deaf and dumb. Well, actually he's not dumb. We just refer to him that way because he's a former IRS agent."

4. A deaf man mashed his finger with a hammer. Then he couldn't find his pencil and pad.

DRUNK

1. Five men came rushing out of the bar toward their car, and I heard one of them say, "You drive, Freddy. You are too drunk to sing."

2. "What did your wife say when you came home intoxicated last night?" "Nothing. I was going to have those two front teeth pulled anyway."

3. "We had a hard time getting married. She wouldn't marry me when I was drunk, and I wouldn't marry her when I was sober."

4. "I'd been drinking and my wife said, "You've had sufficient, you're drunk enough for me." "I said, 'Honey, I'm never drunk enough for you.'"

5. They told my Ozark neighbor that if he wouldn't drink that it would lengthen his days. He said, It's the truth too. I didn't drink last Sunday and it was the longest day of my life.

6. Man come into the bar and ordered three drinks, then three more. The bartender said, "That's not good for you." "I know it; especially with what I've got." "What have you got?" "One dollar."

7. If you have to drink and drive, do it while my math teacher is crossing the road.

8. "Have you finished your drivers test? At least all of the sober ones will tell you they have."

9. The teacher was putting on a demonstration to some first graders. She put a worm in some water and said, "See nothing happens to the worm." Then she put the worm in some alcohol and the worm died. "Now, class, what does this prove?" James held up his hand and said, "If you drink alcohol, you won't have worms."

10. The hitchhiker got a ride, and soon the car got stopped by a cop. The cop said, all is OK, but what are those knives doing in the back seat? I juggle in a circus. He said it looks like weapons to him and he made him get out and prove it. While he was juggling, two drunks pulled up and they looked at each other in amazement. Then one said, "These sobriety checks are getting rougher all the time."

11. A pious man had his Bible and was boarding different buses attempting to convince people to go the way of the Lord. One man who had been drinking too much, came in and sat down at the back of the bus. The man said to him, "Did you know fellow, that you're going straight to hell?" The drunk said, "Oh my. I got on the wrong bus again."

12. After a very wild party, Henry stopped in the bar for one more drink. He ordered drinks for every customer, plus the bartender and himself. After they had all downed their drinks, he announced that he had no money. So the bartender beat him up and threw him in the street. Next day he did the same thing. On the third day he ordered for all of the customers and himself. The bartender said, "Aren't you going to order one for me?" "Oh no. Not you. One drink and you become a raving maniac."

13. An Ozarker was walking in a cemetery a bit intoxicated one dark night and fell in a grave. He tried and tried and couldn't get out. Finally he stopped and just stood there, unbeknown to him that another man had previously done the same thing, and the voice from the other end of the grave said, "You can't get out of here, can you?" But he did!!

14. Th' mountain dew bizness jest ain't what it use' to be 'round h'ar. Mos'

fellers what made it dun' 'cided that it's 'a lots easier to git on giverment welfare. I don't know which is th' mos' respeakable, tho.

15. Have you tried those new self-opening beer cans, or don't you like the taste of blood?

16. A drunk Ozarker entered a bar and asked for a drink. The bartender refused him. "Just to show you I'm not drunk, do you see that one-eyed cat coming in the back door?" The bartender said, "Now I know darn well you're drunk. The cat is going out."

17. A hitchhiker in the hills of the Ozarks was picked up by a hillbilly who pulled a gun on him and ordered him to take a bottle of corn moonshine from the glove compartment of the car. "Drink it," the hillbilly ordered, waving the gun. The hitchhiker took a swallow from the bottle, gasped, gulped, sobbed, blinked, wept, gagged, choked, shuddered, squirmed, and twitched. "All right," the hillbilly said. "Now you take the gun and force me to take a drink."

18. A wife of an alcoholic decided to scare her husband into quitting the bottle once and for all. When he came home drunk, she was waiting for him with a white sheet over her head, making eerie, screeching, ghostly sounds. As he came in, he said, "Who are you?" "I'm the devil." "Shake hands, devil. I married your sister."

19. The lush's wife thought to reform him, so she trailed him to the neighborhood bar, stood up next to him and ordered a slug of whiskey. When she tasted, she spat out, "How can you drink this awful stuff?" "See there honey," he chuckled. "And all these years you thought I was havin' a good time."

20. A car roared off the highway, through a guard rail, over a cliff, somersaulted three times and sailed into a tree. Witnessing the spectacular mishap, a passing motorist stopped and helped the driver from his smashed car, asking, "Good heavens, are you drunk?" "Of course I'm drunk," was the reply, "what do you think I am, a stunt driver?"

21. A redneck hit an Ozarker at the bar and said, "That's a Karate chop from Korea." The Ozarker quietly went outside and came back and hit the redneck and said, "That's a crow bar from Sears."

22. Every morning a Scotchman would order three beers in the pub. Finally the bartender asked, "Why always three beers?" The Scotchman said, "I have two brothers in the U.S.A. and we always drink to each other." One day he only ordered two beers. The bartender said, "I'm sorry to hear about the loss of one of your brothers." He said, "I didn't lose a brother." "Then why only two beers today?" The Scotchman replied, "Because I've quit drinking."

FALSEHOODS

1. Never believe anything until it has been officially denied.

2. If he told you that he can drive that big rig, you want to watch him. He may lie to you again.

3. Jose Rodrigous, a Mexican, was crossing over in the U.S. and robbing banks. Finally a posse followed and caught him. They said, "Jose, if you don't tell us where you buried that money we're going to shoot you right between the eyes."

He couldn't understand English so they got an interpreter. He told the interpreter that it was buried 10 feet north of the city well. The interpreter turned to the posse and said, "Jose Rodrigous is a very brave man. He is ready to meet his maker." (Rick Wheeler.)

4. A girl walking in the park stepped on a frog. The frog begged her to take him home and put him under her pillow, claiming he was a prince turned into a frog by a wicked witch. When she awoke the next morning, lying beside her was a handsome young man. She just couldn't believe it, and neither did her mother or father.

FOOD

Cooking

1. "Do you want some broccoli?" "No, thanks, I've already had some – when I was about eight years old."

2. "I have to go now. I placed an order for $20 worth of groceries and I want to be home when they slip it under the door."

3. "If we had some bacon, we would have bacon and eggs … if we had some eggs.

4. "The dog ate the cake I baked." "Don't worry, I'll get you another dog."

5. The cooking is so bad at our place that the flies got together and fixed the hole in the screen."

6. "Let him have as much chicken as he wants. They're dying faster than we can eat them anyway."

7. "Why don't you stay for dinner? Thanks, but the storm isn't that bad."

8. A "Well Balanced Meal" is a sandwich in each hand.

9. "I've eaten so many TV dinners that if you will look in my eyes at the right time, you'll see Bonanza."

10. "When company drives up, Mom puts us out on the porch with toothpicks in our mouthes."

11. "I went in to buy some eggs and I saw a carton of a dozen eggs. I asked the merchant, 'How do they make chickens sit so close together.'" (Yakoff Smirnoff.)

12. "If you haven't eaten some of Jackie's good cooking, you will never know what a failure Aunt Jeima really was."

13. "You sure have improved on your cooking, honey. Remember our first meal you were fixing, when I came home from work? You were trying to toast marshmallows with a flashlight."

14. Pat and Mike sat down to eat together. When the meat was passed, Pat grabbed the biggest piece. "Sure and that's fine manners," said Mike. "If I had reached first, I would have taken the smallest piece." "Then what's itchin' ye." said Pat. "Ye got it, didn't ye?"

15. To cure any problems, my Grandma thought chicken soup was the thing. I had a Grandpa that thought a half a pint of whiskey would cure anything. So I just combined the two, "Soup and whiskey." I call it "Pullet Surprise."

16. Should vegetarians eat animal crackers?

17. A college pal, Joe, was telling me about his first year at a company that markets American products in the Middle East. "My initial project, a soft-drink account, was terrific but nearly cost me my job," he said. "To avoid language problems, I erected a three-panel storyboard. The first panel depleted a guy drenched in sweat, standing in the desert. The middle panel showed him gulping down a bottle of our soda. And in the third panel, he's fully refreshed with a big smile." "Sounds great," I told him. "What was the problem?" Larry said, "'I didn't know Arabs read right to left." (Jim Walsh.)

Restaurants

1. The belligerent Northerner came into the restaurant and ask, "Do you serve crabs in here?" The Ozark waitress replied, "We serve anybody in here."

2. A long haired and bearded man came into an Ozark restaurant, and the waitress said, "Is that a customer, or did Elvis lose his hound dog."

3. Waiter: "How did you find your steak, sir?" Customer: "It was just luck. I happened to move a piece of potato and there it was."

4. Seven Elevens are open 24 hours a day. They can't teach their help to lock the doors.

5. Two Ozarkers went in to a cannibal restaurant. After looking over the menu, they called the waitress over. "Ma-am, Why is baked Queen $4, roasted King $6, and fried Hillbilly $850? They're not scarce." The waitress replied, "Did you ever try to clean one of 'em?"

6. A young married man ordered breakfast while on a job away from home. He ordered eggs fried hard, the bacon burned to a crisp, and the biscuits scorched black. The waitress said that they had never had an order like that. "Do you want anything else?" "Yes. Frizz up your hair and sit across from me. I'm homesick."

7. A gentleman from the generous West was on his first visit to New York City. On the first night after their arrival, he and his wife went to a well-known restaurant and ate what seemed to them a not very substantial dinner. When the bill came, it totaled $38.45. The man looked again to make sure of what he had read. Then he called the waiter. "Here, you've made a mistake. I've got more money than that!"

8. A man and an attractive woman were having a candlelight dinner at a fine restaurant when the waiter noticed the man slowly sliding out of his chair and under the table. The woman seemed not to notice as her companion disappeared out of sight. "Pardon me, ma'am," the waiter said. "But I think your husband is under the table" "No, he isn't" the woman said, eyeing the waiter calmly. "My husband just walked through the door."

9. He took me out to eat in a fancy restaurant and embarrassed me. At the main part of the meal, he scratched his back with a fork." "Did that embarrass you?" "It sure did. I was so frustrated that I dropped a whole handful of mashed potatoes in my lap."

10. Waitress: "Yes this is really veal. In fact it has just been following the cow." "It was following the cow, but not for milk," said the customer.

24

GOSSIP

1. "I don't like to talk about anybody unless it's good. And boy is this good!!"
2. A lot of trouble in the world is caused by combining a narrow mind and a wide mouth.
3. The ability to speak several languages is an asset, but the ability to keep your mouth shut in one is priceless.
4. One woman to another: "I won't go into all the details; in fact, I've already told you more about it than I heard myself."

INSURANCE

1. A retail merchant got insurance, and that night his store burned. The company suspected arson, but lacking proof they had to be content with a letter. "Dear Sir: We insured your place of business at 4:30 p.m. The fire didn't occur until 10 p.m. So we can close our records, will you kindly explain the delay?"
2. Two hillbillies struck up a conversation on the beach at Miami. One of them said, "I'm here on insurance money. I collected $10,000 for fire damage."

"Me too," the second hillbilly said. "But I got $20,000 for a flood."

"Tell me, how do you start a flood?"
3. After his best sales pitch, a life-insurance agent couldn't get a young couple to purchase a policy. He finally got up to leave and said, "I don't want to scare you, but please sleep on it tonight. If you wake up in the morning, let me know what you think."

LIFE

1. Life does not begin at the moment of conception, or the moment of birth. It begins when the kids leave home and the Parakeet dies.
2. What's the difference in in-laws and out-laws? Out-laws are wanted.
3. I feel sorry for short people when it rains. They're the last to know about it.
4. I will pay my delinquent bill as soon as I get my mother paid off. A note came back: Dear Sir: After checking our records, we have concluded that we have done more for you than your mother ever did; we've carried you for <u>fifteen</u> months.
5. One exasperated guest approached the park attendant and asked, "How come these maps don't have an arrow telling you where you are?"
6. Irate man to city editor: "You printed a notice of my death in last night's paper. "Editor: "That's right. Say, where are you calling from?"
7. Getting caught is the mother of invention.
8. I believe that one out of every four is a little crazy. How do you tell? If four of you are sitting at a table, look at the other three. If they're alright, you're probably the one.
9. NOISY GUEST: "Sir, I'd like to give you a going away present. But you've

got to do your part."

10. I just found out why my wife and I are having such a hard time keeping up with the Joneses. They're on welfare.

11. We live in an apartment that's so high up, they give you three utilities – gas, electricity and oxygen.

12. There is so much pollution in the air that if it weren't for our lungs, there'd be no place to put it.

13. Teamwork pays off. Look at Niagara Falls. Niagara Falls is nothing but a lot of little drips working together.

14. Sign of the times: – Old lie – The check is in the mail.
New lie – I didn't check the e-mail.

15. Do you know the difference between broccoli and a booger? Little kids don't eat broccoli.

16. Culture is roughly anything we do and the monkeys don't. (Groucho Marx)

17. Any club that would accept me as a member, I wouldn't want to join.

18. A bird left his calling card on a woman's head. A friend said, "Do you have any toilet paper?" "No. If I did it wouldn't do any good, because that pigeon is a half a mile from here by now."

19. I gave my son a shotgun. He said, "You could have given me a watch." I told him,"Son, in 25 years when you walk into your bedroom and your wife is in bed with another man, are you going to say, "Your Time is Up? (Yakoff Smirnoff.)

20. A wealthy man died and his wife had a very nice tombstone set at his grave reading "Rest in Peace." The widow assumed she would be fixed for life, but when they read the will, she found out that he had left all his money to his mistress, leaving the widow nothing. The widow was livid. She went to the monument company and asked if another line could be added to the tombstone. They said sure, what do you want added. She said under the "Rest in Peace," please add, "Till We Meet Again." (Darrell Peters)

MOTEL

1. A man in a Mexican Motel complained that two mice were capering in his room. The clerk asked him, "What do you expect for a peso, a bull fight?"

2. An Ozarker to the motel manager, "You call this a continental breakfast? Is this all you could find on this continent?!"

3. INVESTIGATING - There were no rooms in the hotel. The operator said that he could sleep on a cot in the large ballroom, but there was a lady laying on a cot at the other side. "You will have to promise me not to bother her." "Ok, I'll do anything, because I'm so tired." In the middle of the night, he came running in to the desk clerk hollering, "That lady is dead." See. He was investigating.

MUSIC

1. "Are you a singer?" "No, but my sister can hold High C for three minutes." "That's nothing, my aunt Minnie got up to P the other night, and she'd held it for

three hours.!"

2. What key are you playing in? "E." "Sounds like 'L' to me."

3. I play the piano like lightening; never strike the same place twice.

4. Why is music coming from the grave of Ludwig Van Beethoven's 7th symphony, 1770-1827, and the music is playing backwards? "He's decomposing."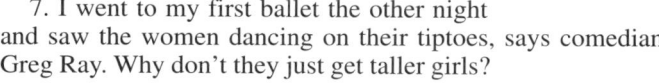

5. Opera: When a guy gets stabbed in the back and instead of bleeding, he sings.

6. A small boy whispered to his mom during the opera performance, "Why is that man threatening the woman on stage with his stick?" "He's not threatening her; he conducts the orchestra," she explained. "Well, if he's not threatening her," the boy replied," then why is she screaming?"

7. I went to my first ballet the other night and saw the women dancing on their tiptoes, says comedian Greg Ray. Why don't they just get taller girls?

OCCUPATIONS

Banker

1. He was going to open a bank here in town, but couldn't get the dynamite.

2. Can anybody tell me why the banks leave the vault open and chain down the ball point pens?

3. A banker wouldn't loan the farmer money. His dog bit the banker, then bit his secretary. "I can sort of understand why he bit me, but why did he bite my secretary?" "To get the bad taste out of his mouth."

4. Most critics are like eunuches in a harem. They know how it is done. They see it done every day, but they are unable to do it themselves.

5. There was a banker who earned over $500,000 dollars a year and attended a large church. It came to the attention of the Elders that the lawyer had never contributed a dime to the church. They appointed a distinguished Elder to talk to the man about it. The lawyer said to the Elder, "I guess you don't know about my mother in the nursing home. It costs 30 to 40 thousand a year for her. "The Elder felt really bad. The banker said, "I guess you didn't know about my sister. Her deadbeat husband left her with six kids and a huge mortgage and no bank account." At this the Elder just shook his head. Then the lawyer said, "I guess too that you didn't know about my brother who is a paraplegic and Medicare and Medicaid don't begin to cover his medical bills. "The elder was almost in tears and said, I can understand why you haven't given to the church" "Given to the church," the banker exclaimed." If I don't give my mother, sister or brother a dime, why do you think I would give to the church?" (Rick Wheeler.)

Blue Collar Worker

1. Henry is one of the best mechanics in his price range.
2. Of all of the mechanics that I ever worked with, I'll have to say that Henry is one of them.
3. I lost my job in the Pork and Beans factory. I put the beans in up side down and gave everybody the hiccups.
4. "What do you do with that great big salary you make?" "Oh, I spend most of it on whisky and wild women, and then I just waste the rest of it.
5. Construction: Man had new house built. Mentioned to architect that it didn't look too strong. "You've got to consider that we don't have the wall paper on yet."
6. A machine in a large plant stopped working, bringing everything to a grinding halt. A repairman was called in. He merely tapped the machine with a hammer and it immediately began working again. When he submitted a bill for $250, the plant manager felt the charge was too high for one little tap of the hammer and demanded the repairman submit a second bill, which he did. It read; "Tapping with a hammer, $1; knowing where to tap, $249."

Business

1. Trying to make a profit today is like being a pickpocket in a nudist camp.
2. Bosses who hire relatives have a payroll that just won't quit!
3. "My wife had her credit card stolen." "That's terrible!" "No, it's not terrible. The thief's spending less then she was."
4. If you can't pay your bills be thankful that you're not one of your creditors.
5. Protect the birds, doves bring peace and storks bring tax exemptions.
6. If it's true that the world is getting smaller, why is the price of a stamp always going up?
7. A budget helps you pay as you go if you don't go anyplace.
8. It is better to give than to lend, and it costs about the same.
9. The board voted to send best wishes to the manager, by a vote of 5 to 4.
10. Blessed are the young, for they shall inherit the national debt.
11. Live within your income and you'll live without worry – and a lot of other things. (Prochnow)
12. We know a family that has no washing machine, no TV, no mink coat – just money in the bank. (Prochnow.)
13. "Your typing is better," said the boss, "but still not good enough for you to stop wearing those tight sweaters."
14. When they audited me, they asked for my personal material. I gave them my diary. They were so entertained that now I get audited every year.
15. It seems that every time you're about to catch up with the Joneses, they refinance.
16. Even if money grew on trees a few smart birds would still get most of it.
17. The partners hired a beautiful young secretary. "Look," said one, "This girl's so pretty and innocent someone may take advantage of her. We should teach her what's right and what's wrong." "Good idea," said the other. "You teach her what's

right."

18. This book is not a novel to be tossed aside lightly. It should be thrown with great force. (Dorothy Parker.)

19. BOOKS – "He writes so well, he makes me feel like putting my quill back in my goose." (Fred Allen.)

20. BOOKS – "Thank you for sending me a copy of your book. I'll waste no time in reading it." (Anon.)

21. IRS commissioner Fred Goldberg has a new simplified tax form; how much money did you make last year? Mail it in."

22. Washington is a city of people doing badly what shouldn't be done at all.

23. On the stock market – Due to the shortage of experienced trumpet players, doomsday will be postponed for three months.

24. There was a bum sleeping behind the bunker at the golf club. The manager gave him a kick amidship, and the bum leaped to his feet and said, "Who are you?" "I'm the manager of the club." "Well, this is sure a heck of a way to get new members."

25. A group of Shiite Moslems came to the U.S. looking for the fastest growing towns in the "Midwest." They chose Branson and West Plains. They spent too much time in Branson and had to hurry to West Plains. When they got here they were introducing themselves differently. I asked them why they weren't introducing themselves as Shiite Moslems. They said while coming over that crooked, hilly 160 highway so fast that bus driver just scared the Shiite out of them. (Pat Cash.)

26. The Ozarker had to complete the information on some insurance papers when he came to the question: "If your father is dead, state the cause." Unwilling to reveal that his father had been hung for cattle-stealing, the lawyer got around the problem by writing: "He died while taking part in a public ceremony when the platform gave way."

27. "To what do you attribute your long life?" the reporter asked the 100 year old man. "I don't rightly know yet," replied the old-timer. "I'm still dickering with two breakfast food companies."

28. Advertising pays. Since Smokey the Bear signs went up in the subways, there hasn't been a single forest fire in New York City.

29. An Ozark woman applied for a charge account at a department store and was asked about her husband's average income. "Usually around midnight," she said.

30. A man protested a tax clerk's ruling that a baby born on January 24 was not deductible on last year's income. "'Why not?" he asked, "It was last year's business?"

Cowboy

1. "You got your saddle on backwards." "How do you know which way I'm going?"

2. Always drink upstream from the herd and don't squat with your spurs on.

3. John Wayne Toilet Paper – So rough and tough that it takes a little hide off of everyone, but won't take any crap off of anybody.

4. While the cowboy was walking through the prairie, a stampede of cattle came after him. He ran and ran, but there was not a tree or a hill in sight. Just as the stampede got to him and was about to trample him to death, he reached up and grabbed a limb and let the cattle go by. "I thought you said there were no trees." "THERE HAD TO BE A TREE."

5. Two men decided to fight a duel with pistols. One of the men was very, very fat, and when he noticed how thin the other man was, he became excited. Fat Man: "I'm twice as big a target as you are! I ought to stand twice as far away from you as you stand from me." The thin man agreed, but somehow they couldn't work it out. So at last the fat man offered a second solution. Taking a piece of chalk from his pocket, he drew two lines down the fat man's coat, leaving a space between them. Second (to thin man) "Now, fire away. But remember, any hits outside the chalk lines don't count."

Doctor

1. I looked in the newspaper ads and got the best doctor that I could find; Dr Pepper. But when I got there, they said he was in the can.

2. I looked in the yellow pages, and it said that the doctor was free on Thursdays.

3. They gave me a jar and said fill it. I said, do you want regular or unleaded.

4. I went to the surgeon and asked him what he could do for me for $500. He said I can send you a get well card.

5. The Dr. said that he would have me walking in 30 days. He kept his promise. I had to sell my car when I got his bill.

6. Some doctors cure heart trouble with shock treatments. They send them out the first of every month.

7. "Doc, that's three times what you usually charge." "I know, but you yelled so loud that you scared away three other patients."

8. When I went in to the operating room, I asked what the death rate was around here. He said,"About one per person."

9. "Then he said, can I help you further?" I said, "Yes, help me get my pants on. I'm getting out of here."

10. A scary surgery is when you hear the nurse say, "Did this patient sign the organ-donor card?" or "everyone stand back, I think I lost a contact."

11. The curtains were drawn and the room was dark when I woke up from my operation, and I asked my wife why? She said the building next door got on fire and we didn't want you to wake up and the first thing look out the window and think your operation was unsuccessful.

12. If I'd have known I'd of had as rough of a time with my operation as I did, I would have gone to Dr. Kavorkin.

13. When I was in the hospital after a car wreck, the nurses would come in every six hours to take my temperature. Sometimes they would take it through the

mouth and some times rectally. I had a broken jaw so I was kinda glad when they wired my mouth shut, because I think they were using the same thermometer.

14. The doctor said, "The best thing for you is to stop whisky, smoking, and chasing wild woman." "Well, doc, what's second best."

15. "Doc, can I climb up the stairs yet?" "Why yes." "Oh, I'm so glad, because I'm sick of climbing up and down that darn drain pipe."

16. I was in the doctor's waiting room and a fellow came out from the Dr. with his toe cut off. I asked him why. He said that he had Ptomaine Poisoning. I accepted that. Pretty soon a man came out with his knee cut off. I ask him why. He said because he had Amnesia. So with that, I just picked up my coat and hat and got out of there, because I knew I had Asthma.

17. A woman was helping her mother fill out a medical form at the doctor's office. The daughter said, "it says here to check your past diseases and ailments. "The mother paused for a moment and replied, "Check them all. I might as well get my money's worth."

18. Doctor, I have had my tongue out, but you haven't looked at it. "Well, at least it kept you quiet while I wrote your prescription."

19. "When I have a headache, I take aspirin. With a cold, I go to bed and drink fluids. With stomach problems, I take bicarbonate of soda. Doc, have I been doing things right," the lady asked? "You've been doing just fine. That'll be $50."

20. Doctor to patient: "Let me know if this prescription works. I'm having the same trouble."

21. Doctor to patient. "The check you gave me came back," "That's nothing, so did my arthritis."

22. Virus is a word used by doctors to mean, "Your guess is as good as mine."

23. Innuendo – Italian for Preparation H.

24. Minor operation: One that is performed on someone else.

25. Mother: "Why can't you behave like that good little girl next door?" Daughter: "She's a doctor's kid; he always keeps the best ones for himself!"

26. Jane said, "Doc., I want a tooth pulled and I don't want any anesthetic because I'm in a hurry." That's very brave of you. Which tooth is it?" "Husband, dear, show him your tooth."

27. "I heard today that your son is an undertaker. I thought you said he's a physician." "Not at all sir. I said he followed the medical profession."

28. Mother: "Now, Junior, be a good boy and say 'ah' so the doctor can get his hand out of your mouth."

29. Epitaph on the grave of the hypochondriac: "I told you I was sick!"

30. "I wouldn't mind hearing about her operation if she'd only stop and listen to mine."

31. I was in bed with 104. Boy was it crowded.

32. Doctor to patient: "I can't quite diagnose your case. It must be the drink." "OK, I'll come back when you're sober enough to do it."

33. What's the bandage for? When he told me to go milk the cows, he didn't tell me we had a bull.

34. Cow manure is good for chapped lips. It won't heal them, but you sure won't lick them.

35. An Ozarker went to the doctor because every time he put on his straw hat he heard music. The doctor told him to remove his 'hat band'.

36. The Doctor came over and examined him. Then he told his wife to keep him in bed, give him lots of bicarbonates, and take some cooking lessons.

37. Jim, bent over and using a cane, was hobbling down the street when his friend Frank saw him and asked, "What's the matter with you?" Jim replied, "I just can't stand up straight." Frank then recommended his doctor. The next week, Frank saw Jim walking in an upright position and asked, "What did the doctor do to get you well in just one week?" "He gave me a longer cane," came the reply.

38. "What is the survival rate of this operation?" The Doctor replied that there are usually 4 or 5 that don't make it,"but I'll do my best." "Is there anything I can do before I begin?" Yes. Help me on with my pants. I'm getting out of here."

39. Taking your medicine is about like asking Dr. Kavorkin for a flu shot.

40. I know that I don't deserve this award, but I have arthritis, and I don't deserve that either.

41. A doctor fuming when finally reaching the banquet table after breaking away from a woman seeking advice. He said to a lawyer setting next to him, "Do you think I should send her a bill?" "Why not? You rendered professional services." "Thanks, I'll just do that." At the office the next morning ready to send the bill, he found a statement from the lawyer. "For Legal Services. $100."

42. The doctor told an Ozarkian that he had terminal cancer and his grandson was with him. Afterwards he met the boys and told them he had AIDS. Going home the grandson said, "Grand Pa, I thought you had cancer." "Well lad, I just told them that so they will let Grandma alone."

43. I'm against anything that might be harmful to your body. I don't even gargle Listerine. It's supposed to kill germs on contact. I don't want something dying in my mouth. (Jim Stafford.)

44. "Doc, tell me in plain words exactly what's wrong with me." "In plain words, you are just lazy," said the doctor. "Now, doctor," the patient replied, "give me the medical term to tell my friends."

45. At the peak of the cold and virus season last winter, our family doctor was giving a record number of penicillin injections. Tacked to the door of his inner office one afternoon was this notice: "To Save Time, Please Back into the Office."

46. "Nurse," said the patient one morning, "I'm in love with you. I don't want to get well." "Don't worry," replied the nurse cheerfully. "You won't. The doctor's in love with me too, and he saw you kissing me this morning!"

47. "Now tell me," said the psychiatrist to his patient, "what did you dream last night?" "Well, doc," answered the patient, settling himself on the couch, "to be honest with you, I didn't dream anything." "How in the world do you expect me to help you," replied the exasperated psychiatrist, slamming his notebook down on the desk, "if you're not going to do your homework?"

48. A man died and went to heaven. St. Peter checked through his book of names and said: ''I can't find your name. Would you please spell it for me?" The man spelled his name, and St. Peter checked his book again. Then he said: "Say! You're not due until 2004. Who's your doctor?"

49. There was the tragic case of the Ozark woman who was determined to end it

all. She called her physician and startled him by asking what was the best way to commit suicide. "What!" asked the medical man, "What on earth do you want to do that for?" "Never mind doctor. I've been too much trouble and my mind is made up. If you don't advise me, I'll just jump off of a high building or something, so you'd better tell me." "Well, if you take it that way," he said, "the best thing to do is to go home, undress, go to bed and shoot yourself two inches below the left breast." The woman took his advice, went home and blew off her knee-cap!

50. A hillbilly called on a surgeon and told him he had been given a handsome set of cuff links for his birthday, but did not own a single shirt with French cuffs. "Why did you come to me" asked the doctor. "I'd like to get my wrist's pierced," the hillbilly replied.

51. Grandpa's just got one ear. He can still hear, but just catches every other word.

52. Isn't it a bit unnerving that doctors call what they do "practice"?

53. When you open a bag of cotton balls, is the top one meant to be thrown away?

54. He went to the doctor to take a small wart off of his arm. The nurse said, "Go down the hall, go in the first door on the right and take off all of your clothes." He said, "That sure is a mean nurse," to the fellow who was already in the room with his clothes off. The other fellow said, "She sure is. I'm just the UPS man."

54. A sick man went to a doctor he hadn't visited before. As he entered the office, he noticed a sign: "$20 first visit, $10 subsequent visits." To save a few bucks, he greeted the doctor by saying, "Nice to see you again." The doctor nodded his hello, then began the exam. His expression turning grave as he poked and prodded the ill man. "Doc, what is it?" the patient asked. "What should I do?" "Well," the doctor said, setting his stethoscope down, "Just keep doing the same thing I told you to do last time you were here."

Employee

1. An elderly gentleman called at a city office on the afternoon of a big baseball game, and said to the principal: "I think my grandson, Peter Smith, is employed here. May I speak to him for a few minutes?" "I'm sorry, but he's gone to attend your funeral."

2. Caller: "Are you sure the manager is not in?" Office boy: "Do you doubt his word, sir??"

3. There must be something to reincarnation – judging by the way some people come back to life at quitting time.

4. But women really have it made today. You hire a secretary and you wind up paying her to learn how to spell while she's looking for a husband.

5. Office Caller: "How long has that office boy worked for you?" Chief Officer: "Oh, about four hours." Caller: "Four hours! Why, I thought he'd been here a long time." Chief: "Oh yes, he's been here two years."

6. Would-be employer: "Have you any-references?" Would-be Employee: "Sure, here's a letter: "To whom it may concern: John Jones worked for us one week and we're satisfied."

7. The boss returned from lunch in a good humor, and called in the whole staff to listen to a couple of jokes he had picked up. Everybody but one girl laughed uproariously. "What's the matter?" grumbled the boss. "Haven't you a sense of humor?" "I don't have to laugh," said the girl. "I'm leaving on Friday, anyhow."

8. The Ozarker sent the young boy he had hired to the pump to get a bucket of water. He came back with the bucket but forgot the water. The Old Ozarker said, "Son, you'd forget your rear if it wasn't tied to you."

9. "Why are you late?" "I overslept" You mean you sleep at home as well."

10. I feel about as out of place as a: Logger at a quilting bee. Cowboy dancing the ballet. Eskimo at a nudist colony. A fan dancer in a convent.

Farming

1. It's so dry here in the Ozarks that the trees are following the dogs around.

2. I am in favor of Day Light Saving Time. My tomatoes do much better with that extra hour of sunlight.

3. A bumper sticker read; Keep your car doors locked! This is zucchini season.

4. An Ozarker was overheard saying that the ground was so poor around here that the only black dirt we have is where we change oil on the old pickup.

5. I lost my old crushed hat in the cow pasture. I went to look for it and I tried on 8 or 10 before I found the right one. (Pat Cash)

6. Two turkey gobblers visiting, "See you after the Holidays. I hope."

7. Tenderfoot: "How can I tell mushrooms from toadstools? Second Class Scout: "Eat some before you go to bed. If you wake up the next morning, they're mushrooms."

8. Shopping for plants in a new garden center, we asked an employee whether the store offered any kind of guarantee if the plants didn't survive. "Oh, yes," he responded, "It's printed on the back of our receipts." Satisfied, we completed our purchase and left. It wasn't until we got home that we actually read the receipt. It stated: We guarantee our plants to grow – or die trying.

9. The Ozarker that lived way back in the hills made his first trip to town and kicked on the sidewalk. This is the first time I've seen dirt that hard. I don't blame them for building a town here. This ground's too hard to plow anyway.

10. Top price for the day at a recent auction was reached when the auctioneer shouted, "Sold to the little lady with her husband's hand over her mouth."

11. To tell wanted plants from weed, pull both kinds out. Those that come up again are weeds!

12. A fellow carrying two chickens in a sack met an Ozarker. "If you can tell me how many chickens are in this sack, I'll give you both of them." "Five?" the hillbilly replied.

13. The wealthy old farmer looked around the dinner table at his strapping young sons and their attractive wives. "I don't see any grandchildren here," he observed. "I want you to know I'll give $50,000 to the first couple to present me with a grandchild. And now, we'll say grace." He bowed his head in prayer...and when he

raised it a moment later, he and his wife were alone at the table.

14. Did you hear about the tree surgeon who fell out of his patient?

15. Do you know why the chewing gum crossed the road? Because it was stuck to the chicken.

16. Do you know why the chicken crossed the playground? To get to the other slide.

17. There was the fellow who always called a spade a spade until the other day when he hit his foot with one.

18. The New Yorker asked why have a tractor with no seat or steering wheel. The farmer said, "That's for an Ozarker who has lost his hind end and don't know which way to turn."

19. A traveling salesman asked an Ozarker what he did with all of those chain saws he'd been buying from him anyway. "I sells them." "How much do you get for them?" "Ah gets hunert feefty." "You must be stupid. You pay more than that." "Beats farming though."

20. Mrs. Newlywed was determined that the grocer should not take advantage of her inexperience. "Don't you think these eggs are rather small?" she asked critically. "Indeed I do," agreed the grocer. "but that's the kind the farmer sends me. They were fresh from the country this morning." "Yes," said the shopper, "that's the trouble with the farmers. They're so anxious to sell their eggs they take them out of the nests before they're ripe."

Flying

1. An Ozarker got a job in an airport and a customer asked him why that mistletoe was hanging over the luggage rack? He said, "So you can kiss your luggage "goodbye."

2. Both engines went out. The pilot came walking through the passenger cabin wearing a parachute, saying, Don't worry folks, I'm going for help.

3. My boss mentioned that all our business travel was wearing him down. I said, "Einstein theorizes that as a body approaches the speed of light, it ages at a slower rate. So the more time you spend on jets, the slower you'll age." "Interesting," my boss said pensively. "But did Einstein take into account airline food?"

4. Two women were preparing to board an airliner. One of them turned to the pilot and said, "Please don't go faster than sound; we want to talk."

5. A C-37 was far up in the sky when the pilot began to laugh hysterically. "What's the joke?" asked a passenger. "I'm thinking what they'll say at the asylum when they find out I've escaped."

6. Airplane Passenger: "How're we doing?" "Pilot: "We're lost, but we're making good time."

7. They have to recycle urine on the Russian Space Ship in order to get water. If you think Tang tastes bad before!

8. Then there was the old lady in the Ozarks who said, "They'll never get me into an airplane. Flying is against human nature. I'm going to stay here on the ground and watch television like the Good Lord intended me to."

35

9. An Ozarker was going to take his first airplane ride until he arrived at the Will Rogers Airport, the only airport named after someone killed in a plane wreck, which is next to the Amelia Airheart Training Center.

10. A pretty stewardess on a Washington-Miami flight had her hands full, fending off two drunks who would not let up. One seated in front of the plane was doing his best to persuade her to come to his apartment. At the rear, the second drunk was trying for an invitation to her apartment. As the plane headed for the runway, the front-seat pest handed her a key and a slip of paper on which he had written his address. "Here's the key and my address," he whispered. "See you tonight?" "Okay," she whispered back with a smile as she headed for the drunk at the rear. She handed him the key and slip of paper and said, "Don't be late."

11. A woman entered a plane with a newborn infant in her arms. A drunk sat down next to her. He took one look at the baby and said, "Ma'am, I've never seen anything more repulsive in my life. Your baby is the ugliest thing I've ever set eyes on." The mother, livid with rage, rang for the stewardess. "Miss," she said, "I've never been so insulted in my life. Either you get this obnoxious wretch away from me, or I'll sue the airline for every penny it has. Diplomatically, the stewardess led the drunk to another seat in the rear of the plane. Then she rushed back to the lady passenger. "I'm terribly sorry this had to happen," she explained. "Now you just relax. I'll bring you a hot cup of coffee and I'll dig up a banana for your monkey."

Lawyers

1. Why are they using lawyers for lab animals now? Because they are more plentiful and you don't get quite so attached to them.

2. Do you know why N.J. has more garbage dumps, and N.Y. has more lawyers? N.J. got first choice. (Scott Foster.)

3. Do you know why they bury lawyers 9 feet deep? They're good fellows "Way Down Deep."

4. How many lawyers does it take to grease a combine? One, if you run him through fast enough.

5. One attorney to another: "I believe a man is innocent until he runs out of money."

6. "How bad are you hurt?" "I don't know. I haven't seen my lawyer yet."

7. "Have you got a lawyer yet? "No, I've just decided to tell the truth."

8. A jury – 12 people decide who has the best lawyer.

9. Did you hear about the terrorists who took a courthouse full of lawyers hostage? They threatened to release one lawyer every hour unless their demands were met.

10. A wise old judge was once asked to settle a dispute between two brothers about the fair division of a large estate left them by their father. "Let one brother divide the estate," he ruled, "and let the other have first choice."

11. The judge had just passed sentence when he heard the accused muttering vigorously. "What's that?" demanded the judge. "It sounded like cussing." "Nossir,

not on your life," said the defendant. "All I said was 'God am the judge, God am the judge'."

12. The Hollywood starlet on the witness stand didn't seem to care how much of her famous chassis was exposed to the jury. As her dress seemed to inch higher and higher, the prosecuting attorney said, "Point of order, your honor, I just thought of something." "Of course you have," said the judge. "So has everyone else in the courtroom."

13. I know a fella who just sent out 40,000 Valentine cards doused in French perfume and signed "GUESS WHO?" He's a divorce lawyer.

14. If Christ would return now, He'd kick the lawyers out of the temple.

15. In heaven a lawyer got an extra fancy castle. The Pope only got a small simple room. Lawyer felt inadequate and asked why he got such a good place? We have many Popes here, but you're the only lawyer we've had.

16. Walking into a lawyer's office, a man asked what the barrister's rates were. "Fifty dollars for three questions," the lawyer stated. "Isn't that awfully expensive?" the man asked. "Yes," the lawyer replied. "What's your third question?"

17. Four surgeons were taking a coffee break and comparing notes. "I think accountants are the easiest to operate on," the first one said. "You open them up and everything is numbered." "I think librarians are the easiest to operate on," the second one offered. "You open them up and everything inside is in alphabetical order." The third one said, "I like engineers - they always understand when you have parts left over at the end." "I prefer to operate on lawyers," said the fourth surgeon, the most experienced of the group. "They're heartless, spineless and gutless, and their heads and rear ends are interchangeable."

Outlaws

1. Little boy asked his dad, "Who are those pictures on the Post Office wall?" "They are hardened criminals who are wanted by the FBI," his dad told him. The little boy said, "Why didn't they keep them when they took their pictures."

2. A German, a Frenchman, and an American banker was going to be beheaded. They were all asked if they wanted their heads down or up facing the guillotine. They all chose looking up. The German went first and the guillotine stuck. As a result the rules were that he should be released free. The Frenchman went second and the same thing happened and he was released. The banker went last and as he was looking up, the same thing was about to happen when he said, "Oh, wait a minute boys. I see the problem."

Police

1. Annoyed driver to patrolman who has pulled her over. Why can't you people get organized? One day you take my license away, and the next day you ask to see it.

2. Patrolman writing ticket kept swatting flies. He said, "What kind of flies are

those?" Passenger said, "Circle flies." "Why circle flies?" Because they only circle around "horses' butts." "Look fellow. Are you referring to me as a "horses rear?" "No, I'm not sir. But you sure can't fool those flies."

3. Why didn't you settle this case out of court? That's just what we were doing when the police separated us.

4. "Well, well, so you're lost" said the kindly policeman to the frightened little boy. "Why didn't you hang on to your mommy's skirt?" "I tried" sobbed the little fellow, "but I couldn't reach it."

5. Someone came into the police department and stole all of the toilets. They cannot solve that problem. They have nothing to go on. (Yakoff Smirnoff.)

6. A prisoner was complaining about having to march 10 miles in the jungle during 100 degree temperatures to face a firing squad. "Why are you complaining, said the warden? We have to walk back."

7. Driving to work, I had to swerve to avoid a box that fell out of the truck in front of me. Moments later, a trooper pulled me over for reckless driving. Luckily, another patrolman had seen the object in the road, so they stopped traffic and retrieved the box, which turned out to contain large upholstery tacks. "I'm sorry, sir," said the first trooper, "but I'm going to have to write you a ticket after all. "For what?" I asked, surprised. He replied, "Tacks evasion."

8. "You didn't stop at that stop sign." Ozarker: But I slowed down." "It's against the law; you're supposed to stop." "But I slowed down. What's the difference?" "He grabbed me around the neck and started beating me with a flashlight." "I told him to stop and he said, "Do you want me to stop or just to slow down." (Pat Cash.)

9. If the cops arrest a mime, do they tell him he has the right to remain silent?

Politics

1. In the first place, God made idiots. That was for practice. Then he made politicians.

2. America – a place where we go on the air to kid politicians and where politicians go on the air to kid us.

3. Al Gore – Remember when the air was clean and sex was dirty.

4. Notice that most of the people favoring abortion have already been born.

5. Many a man's honesty has saved him from becoming a politician.

6. Dick Armey about Democrats: "One must, it's true, forgive one's enemies. But not before they have been hanged."

7. I always get two groups in Washington, D.C. confused. One is the Ways & Means Committee. The other is the Internal Revenue Service – the Ways To Be Mean Committee.

8. It's getting harder and harder to support our government in the style to which it has become accustomed.

9. A politician who had changed his views rather radically was congratulated by a colleague. "I'm glad you've seen the light," he declared. "I didn't see the light," the politician replied, "I felt the heat."

10. You can't loose. The Lord helps those who help themselves, and the Government helps those who won't.

11. Two Americans were lost on a desert island. "Don't worry," said one. "They'll rescue us. They'll find us. They'll pick us up." "How can you be so sure?" asked the other. Said the first: "I haven't paid my income tax."

12. Wouldn't it be wonderful if the mini-skirt designers were in charge of government budgets?

13. A state official died and at his funeral an office-seeker got the governor aside and asked if he could have the dead man's place. "I have no objection," said the governor, "if the undertaker will agree."

14. Roared the politician to the editor: "What do you mean by publicly insulting me in your old rag of a paper? I will not stand for it, and I demand an immediate apology!" "Just a moment," answered the editor. "Didn't the news item appear exactly as you gave it to us – that you had resigned as city treasurer?" "It did, but where did you put it? In the column under the heading, 'Public Improvements!'

15. One party can't fool all of the people all of the time. That's why we have two parties.

16. We could wipe out the National Debt if there was a tax on campaign promises.

17. About cattle prices being so low: You can't fall out of bed when you're sleeping on the floor.

18. Columbus was the first great politician; He didn't know where he was going. When he got there, he didn't know where he was. When he got back, he didn't know where he had been; and he did it all on somebody's money.

19. If there is anyone in the sound of my voice that opposes this matrimony, speak now or forever hold your peace. "There was a moment of silence and Old Uncle John got up in the back of the church and said, "If no one is going to use this time, I would like to say a few words for Bill Clinton."

20. A Russian father was discussing his three sons: "I'm very proud of them. One is a people's lawyer and one's a people's doctor. But I'm proudest of all of my son who is in America. He's unemployed and gets money from the government...and if it weren't for the few dollars he sends home, we'd all starve.

21. For years the sideshow strong man had awed the crowds by squeezing a lemon dry, then offering $1,000 to anybody who could get another drop out of it. Nobody paid much attention when a wispy little man in the audience dared to challenge him. The strong man first squeezed the lemon until it was little more than a pulp, then handed it to the little man, who not only squeezed out another drop, but quite a bit more juice out of it. "Amazing!" gasped the strong man. "What kind of work do you do?" Replied the little man: "I'm with the Internal Revenue Service."

22. The two men seated together on a long train trip were unacquainted, but one finally spoke to the other saying: "I was just released from prison this morning. It's going to be a tough job to face old friends." "I know what you mean," said the other, "I'm just getting home from Congress."

23. President Clinton has a great routine. He gets into his plane and tells the pilot: "Go anywhere; we got troubles all over."

24. Two women meet in the street. Says the first, "I remember your son, Mark, was trying so hard to get a job with the federal government. What is he doing now?" Says the second: "Nothing. He got the job."

25. Nowadays one has to be very careful with political jokes, because many times political jokes get elected.

26. Scandal may be a good thing – It's got a lot of politicians to admit they know nothing.

27. Critics say that Washington isn't very good at secret intelligence. I think they've done a great job of keeping their intelligence secret.

28. When I was presiding judge of the Third Judicial Circuit Court of South Dakota, my administrative assistant accompanied me on occasional trips throughout the circuit. One time, I was buckling myself into the passenger seat of her new car when I asked, "Does this car have an air bag on my side?" She smiled and said, "It does now." (Dale Bradshaw.)

29. Two friends were discussing their family histories when one of them lamented that he knew precious little about his roots. I've always wanted to have my family history traced," he said, "but I can't afford to hire someone. Any suggestions?" "Sure," replied his friend. "Run for public office." (Earle Hitchner.)

President Clinton

1. "I'm president of the U.S. and I have my wife's permission to say so."

2. Bill Clinton's approval rating is up to 50%. If it gets up to 60%, he can start dating again.

3. Bill Clinton said to send him candy. He's had Flowers for 10 years.

4. Every place usually has something they enjoy making fun of. Arkansas had one person they wanted to get rid of and they did; and her husband too.

5. George Washington never told a lie; Nixon never told the truth; and Bill Clinton can't tell the difference. (Pat Cash.)

6. It shows how styles have changed. George Washington was referred to as The Father of our Country. Nowadays they refer to President Clinton as some kind of a son.

7. We don't need to build a fence around U.S. now to keep illegal aliens out. We've elected Bill Clinton again.

8. The doctor was going to check my heart, and I told him to just take it out. "I can get along without a heart. Bill Clinton does."

9. An Ozarker said to a Texan that it was too bad that Bill Clinton raised taxes, and the Texan hit him. The Ozarker said, "Why did you hit me? I just wanted to be friendly. I just said that it was too bad that Bill Clinton raised taxes. The Texan said, "Oh I'm sorry. I thought you said that Bill Clinton was raised in Texas."

10. President Clinton was real happy at Christmas time. He thought he saw the three Wise Men coming across the White House Lawn. But it wound up just being the investigating committee.

Preachers

1. A Hillbilly sister to the new preacher, "Preacher, we never knew what sin was until you come."

2. The preacher said to the Hillbilly sister, "Sister Smith, I think adultery is just as bad of a sin as murder, don't you?" She puffed on her pipe a while and finally said, "I don't reckon I rightly know, Parson, I ain't never kilt nobody."

3. Old preachers never retire, they just go out to pastor.

4. My wife really doesn't come out and say it was a bad sermon, but while she's in town I read her diary.

5. The difference between a good sermon and a poor one is a nap.

6. The length of a sermon depends on whether you are awake or asleep.

7. A good sermon helps people in different ways: some rise from it strengthened, others wake from it refreshed.

8. The man who walks in his sleep should get back before the sermon is finished.

9. If you want to hear one man talk and keep 50 women silent, go to church.

10. The hat was passed in a tight-fisted congregation one Sunday morning. It returned almost completely empty. "Oh, Lord," the preacher reverently intoned, "I thank thee that I got my hat back."

11. "Preacher, why did you leave your last job?" "Sickness. The church was sick of me."

12. The little daughter of a clergyman stubbed her toe and cried out, "Darn!" "I'll give you 10 cents if you never use that word again," her father said. A few days later, the little girl came to him and was quite excited. "Daddy," she said, "I've got a new word that's worth half a dollar."

13. A baby started crying during the sermon and the minister quickly responded with, "I didn't know I could move my audience to tears so quickly."

14. Preacher: "Do you want to go to Heaven?"
    Ozarker: "No, Sir."
    Preacher: "Of course you want to go to Heaven when you die."
    Ozarker: "Oh sure, when I die. I thought you were getting up a party to go now."

15. After a very positive meeting a group of preachers went to a restaurant and there were a couple of comical parsons who among them had the whole group laughing as they entered the door. They kept telling stories and laughing, and finally one went up to order and the proprietor said, "Oh, I know what your kind wants. I have them in here like you all of the time. You want pepperoni and a pitcher of beer." The preacher said, "We don't need the pepperoni." (Rick Wheeler.)

16. When his wife was gone, the preacher found a box under the bed with three eggs and $2,000 in it. She explained it to him. Every time he had a bad sermon she put an egg in the box. "Have I only had three bad sermons and why the money?" "Every time I get a dozen eggs, I sold them."

17. He asked me if I was one of those narrow Baptists who think only Baptists are going to Heaven. I'm narrower than that. I don't believe half of them are going to make it.

18. Preacher's voice increasingly woke the baby and it started crying. The young mother started to the door with the baby and the preacher said, "Sister Smith, you don't need to take that baby out, he ain't bothering me none." "Maybe he ain't Parson, but you sure are bothering the heck out of him."

19. When the minister was reading his resignation, a lady in the front of the sanctuary begin crying. He walked over to her and asked her why she was crying. "Because of your leaving," she said. The minister tried to comfort her in saying, "Don't worry, you may even like the next one better." She cried harder and said, "That's what they said last time."

20. Pastor answered the phone the day before Christmas, and he recognized the voice as one of the deacons. "Please send me a quart of scotch and a fifth of gin tonight." "This is the pastor." "Pastor, what are you doing in a liquor store?"

21. A man had a very mean brother that died. He tried hard to get someone to preach his funeral that would call him a Saint, but they all refused. Finally a preacher accepted. At the service he made the following remark, "This man was no good, but compared to his brother, he was a Saint."

22. The preacher spoke for an hour and ten minutes. Before it ended, an elder got up to leave. The usher asked him where he was going. He said to get a haircut. The usher said, "Why didn't you get a haircut before you came?" The elder replied, "I didn't need one then." (Rick Wheeler.)

23. A Church of Christ and a Campbellites attended the same church and couldn't agree on the piano. One Sunday it would be there and the next Sunday it wouldn't. On one Sunday it was completely gone. After six months they found it. It was in the baptistery.

24. A little boy traded his lawn mower to a preacher for a bicycle. Later as the little boy rode his bicycle by the preacher's house he noticed that the preacher couldn't get the lawn mower started. The preacher told him that he sold him a bunch of junk. The little boy told him that as you cranked it, you've got to cuss. The preacher said, "Well son, I've been a preacher for 30 years and I don't cuss. In fact I can't even remember a single cuss word." The little boy said, "Well preacher, you just crank on that thing for about 30 minutes and your memory will come back to you."

25. To the minister–Do you always get enough sleep? Not as much as my audiences.

Salesman

1. SALES – In salesmanship, a foot in the door is worth two on the desk.

2. SELLING – First Salesman: I made some very valuable contacts today. Second Salesman: I didn't get any orders either.

3. Real estate salesmen to the couple, "This is truly a restricted development. No one is allowed to build a house he can afford."

4. Clerk: What terms would you like?
Customer: I'll pay cash.
Clerk: Cash! I'll have to get the manager to see how to handle this.

5. A customer wanted to buy a 5 pound chicken. The merchant only had one

chicken left. He weighed it and said it was exactly 5 pounds. The customer then said, on second thought I'd rather have a 7 pound chicken. The merchant weighed it again and said that it was exactly 7 pounds. Then the customer said, "By the way, I think I'll just take them both."

6. A man saw a suit hanging outside a pawnbroker's shop with a $5.00 price ticket on it. He took it off the hook and carried it inside the shop. Man: How much is this worth? The pawnbroker gave it a disparaging look and said: Not more than $2.00. Man: I'll take it. Pawnbroker: Take it? I thought you were selling it!

7. The man leaned on the drug store counter, lighted his cigar and started to puff away. "Please stop that," said the druggist, "we don't permit smoking." "Why, I just bought this cigar here" the smoker exclaimed. "Look," said the druggist, "we also sell laxatives."

Show Business

1. Johnny Carson is going to take his 4th wife – The first three took him.

2. He is entitled to get married again. He still has a couple of houses left.

3. How come Ed McMahon is the one who drinks, and Doc dresses like he's had too much. (Bob Hope.)

4. Today, watching television often, means fighting, violence and foul language – and that's just deciding who gets to hold the remote control. (Donna Gephart.)

5. During a recent vacation in Las Vegas, I went to see a popular magic show. After one especially amazing feat, a man from the back of the theater yelled, "How'd you do that?" "I could tell you, sir," the magician answered. "But then I'd have to kill you." After a short pause the man yelled back, "Okay, then – just tell my wife!" (Suzanne Oliver.)

6. I was going to juggle knives, but I lost my job to Lorena Bobbitz.

7. Lorena Bobbitz is a marketing specialist for Crisco – a shortening expert.

8. My uncle was a high diver in the circus. He's dead now though. He climbed a 50-foot tower and jumped into a 50-gallon tank of water. That didn't kill him though. In the second part of the act, he climbed a 50-foot tower and jumped into a 5-gallon bucket of water. That didn't kill him either. In the third part of the act, he climbed a 50-foot tower and jumped into a wet wash cloth. And that didn't kill him. What killed him was that somebody rung out the wash rag.

Undertaker

1. "Do you believe in the survival of the fittest?" "I don't believe in the survival of anybody, I'm an undertaker."

2. If the funeral procession is at night, do folks drive with their headlights off?

OCEAN

1. On my wife's first visit to the sea shore, she saw a man in a boat and purchased a bottle of sea water from him to show her friends back home. He charged her $2 for it. A few hours later she returned and the tide had gone out. She commented to the man in the boat, who was naturally farther out in the ocean; "Say

you've sure done a good business today."

2. An Ozark lady said that she almost ran over a man from Miami today. How did you know he was from Miami? When he reached the sidewalk, I heard him say something like, "Sun on a Beach."

3. An Ozarker, after finishing his job in a bathroom in the big city, said, "Who in the heck wound all this here paper around this COB?"

OZARKS

1. Do you know how to tell a rich Ozarkian from a poor one? The rich one has two cars jacked up in his front yard.

2. Do you know what an Ozark credit card is? – A siphon hose.

3. If you get there before I do, you make a blue mark. If I get there before you do, I'll rub it out.

4. The driver of the wagon, going down a steep Ozark hill, said to his northern passengers, "Are you afraid of hills? If you are, just close your eyes. That's what I'm going to do."

5. Down here in the Ozarks, we live in a land where there are two rocks to one dirt. And the only crop rotation we have is just turn the rock over and plant on the other side.

6. Land is so cheap down here that you have to watch the Real Estate Agent, or he will slip an extra forty acres in on you.

7. Our best crop here in the Ozarks is New Comers. And we're always ready for a new harvest.

8. The population of our town never changes. Every time a new baby is born, somebody leaves town.

9. An Ozarker built three swimming pools; one hot, one cold and one empty. He said, "You see a lot of folks can't swim."

10. Cheating in history class is like trying to smuggle daylight past a rooster.

11. We put up a little building, and my wife and I couldn't agree whether to call it a house or a shed. So we just called it a "Shed House." (Roy Keppie.)

12. In the Ozarks some of our toilets don't flush; they suck. Take caution, because the suction could be a hazard to your assets. (Pat Cash.)

13. The rain is pretty spotty. It's so spotty that I had my double barreled shotgun leaning up against a tree, and it rained one barrel full, and didn't put a drop in the other.

14. I went down to the river and hung my clothes on a limb. Jumped in the water to take a little swim. I laid my shoes in the grass. Jumped in the water clear up to

my – (Knees). Well, that didn't rhyme, but it would have if the water had of been deeper.

15. Ozark directions: Go to the end of the driveway. Then turn right around and come straight back, and it will be the third house on the right.

16. If you get lost in the Ozarks, just keep going and you will soon be back where you started.

17. People from Kansas tell us that the roads in the Ozarks seem to go more uphill than down.

18. My grandson, Scott and I were traveling through the Ozarks and I happened to ask him if he knew just where we were. He looked around a bit and said, "We're lost, but we're still making good time."

19. They named a town in Arkansas after me, "Bald Knob."

20. The reason he had so many kids was that Grand Ma was hard of hearing. In the evening both would be sitting out on the porch in the rocking chairs and Grand Pa would say, Ma are you ready to go to bed, or what?" Grand Ma would shout, "WHAT?"

21. Don't laugh at him, you might give birth to something just like him.

22. A Northerner wanted a cold drink from one of these crystal clear Ozark Springs. He asked a native if that cup was sanitary. The native said, "Reckon so. Everybody uses it."

23. A thirsty Ozarker came to a water hole and started drinking. An Indian boy remarked to him that it was much clearer over here. It doesn't matter, he said. I intend to drink it all.

24. An Ozarker got down and out and neighbors were bringing in food and supplies. One neighbor came in and said, "Uncle John, I brought you a load of corn." "Oh, thank you. Is the corn shelled?"

25. An Ozarker went to the great beyond, and the first question he asked St. Peter was, "Where's the Welfare Office?" "Why, there's no Welfare Office up here." "No Welfare Office? This is hell, isn't it."

26. Can't take your $5 bet. I saw him jump off the building on the 6 p.m. news. "That's OK," said the Ozarker, "I saw it too, but I didn't think the darn fool would jump again."

27. I put my money in toilet paper and revolving doors. I got wiped out before I could turn around.

28. One Ozarker feels the worst part of doing nothing is that you can never take a day off.

29. You get used to most anything you have to do, that is if you don't know anything else. Like if you live in the Ozarks.

30. If he told you to jump off of a cliff headfirst, would you do it? "Not again."

31. An Ozark lady went into town and a strange man came close to her and she said, "Don't you molest me." He said, "With a pig under your arm, and anvil under the other arm, a pan in your hand, and a chicken in the other one, how could I molest you?" She replied, I could lay the pig on the ground, put the pan on top of the pig, lay the anvil on top of the pan, and I could hold the chicken."

32. Two Ozarkers were being hanged and they were hanging them over the river. When hanging the first one, the knot came undone and he swam to shore.

The second one said, "You better watch how you tie that knot, because I can't swim a lick."

33. If you hear of someone Smoking Pot in the Ozarks, it means that his outhouse is on fire.

34. A Texan ask his Ozark cousin why it took him so long to get down there. He said that he saw a sign that said, "Clean Rest Rooms". We must have cleaned 40 rest rooms on the way down here.

35. An Ozarker was so conservative that he shut the grandfather clock off at night while he was sleeping. One night he said, Ma, you forgot to shut the clock off. OK, I'll go shut it off. No, lay still. It would be more wear and tear on the sheets on the bed than it will be on the clock. (Senator Emery Milton.)

36. A surprise or being startled will sometimes stop the hiccups. A tourist ask the druggist if he had anything to cure the hiccups. The druggist just hauled off and slapped him. He staggered backwards and said, "What occasion did you have to hit me?" The druggist said, "Well, you don't have the hiccups anymore, do you?" He replied, "No, I don't, but my wife out in the car still does."

37. They're changing all of the phone systems around now. The other night I made a call to Chicago, and when I finished, I ask the operator what the charges were. She said, "That will be five dollars sir." I said, "Five dollars? Why ma-am, down here in the Ozarks, we can call to hell and back for five dollars." She said, "Yes sir, but down there, that's a local call."

38. An Ozarker was coon hunting and fell off of a steep cliff. As he was falling, he caught a limb with both hands. Pretty soon he hollered out, "Is anyone up there that can help me?" A loud voluminous voice came down, I CAN HELP YOU. Who are you? I AM THE LORD. What do you want me to do Lord. TURN LOOSE OF THAT LIMB. After a short hesitation, he called out, "Is there anyone else up there."

39. The kids threw a hand grenade under the old outhouse. They didn't know that their 90-year-old grandma was in it. She came out of it all dusty and dirty and said, "Glad I didn't do that in the house."

40. A man visiting from Chicago, by the name of Cobb, was being harassed by an Ozarkian by the name of Alec. The man said, "Listen son, do you know what we do with smart Alecs in the city?" The boy said, "Do you know what we do with Cobb's in the country?"

41. "Do you remember when we ran out of gas late one night way down in the Ozarks and we stayed all night with that widow woman? You slept in the house and I slept in the barn." Yes, I remember." "Did you happen to tell her that you was me?" "Yes. Why?" "Well, I got a letter from her lawyer. She passed away and left me the whole farm."

42. A traveling salesman broke down while traveling late at night in the Ozarks. He walked a long way and finally came on to a farm house. He asked the farmer if he could use the telephone." "The Ozarker said, "Why feller, we don't have any phones down here?" "Well, would you have a place that I could sleep, because I'm real tired." "Yes, you can either sleep in the house or out in the hay loft. If you sleep in the house, you'll have to sleep with the baby though." He said he sure didn't want to sleep with any baby so he took the barn. The next morning as he was washing up in the cattle trough, the most beautiful girl that he had ever seen came

out. He said, "Well. Who are you?" She said, "Ah, they call me b-a-b-y. And who are you?" "I'm the darn fool that slept in the barn last night."

43. Genie in the bottle: "Thanks for rescuing me. For that I'll give you any wish that you want." "OK, I want all of the roads in the Ozarks to be level and straight." "Do you realize how much that would cost? "Want me to make another wish?" "Yes." "OK, make me smart enough to have all of the answers for these people I'm going to talk to." "Did you want these roads two lane or four lane?"

44. A Northern family camps in the Ozarks every spring. They have a teenage daughter that just loves this country. Every morning she has to take a stroll over her favorite path, up the hills and valleys, and she has to cross Jacks Fork River on her route. One warm spring day, as she crossed the river, she wanted to take a swim, but she didn't have her swimming suit. After thinking about it, she felt since she was 15 miles from the nearest town, that it would be safe to go skinny dipping just once. So when she had finished her swim, she looked over and saw one of those Ozark boys sitting on the gravel bar on her clothes. She couldn't get him to leave. She was just infuriated. Finally she remembered an old dish pan sticking in the gravel that had probably washed down by a flood. So she picked up the pan and draped it over her front, and came walking out toward the boy and pointing her finger. She said, "Do you know what I think, farmer boy?" He said, "Yah, I know what you think. You think there's a bottom in that dish pan!!"

45. Tourist: "What's the speed limit through this quaint village?" Native: "There ain't none. You city folks can't get through here fast enough to suit us."

46. When I was a small kid, our bathroom caught fire. But we were lucky...it didn't reach the house.

47. In the Depression years, we were so poor that I was 10 years old before I found out that Alpo was a dog food.

48. "Is that the sun or moon?" I don't know, I don't live around here."

49. Jack: "This liniment makes my arm smart." Pat: "Then why not rub some on your head?"

50. LANGUAGE – "It's me" and "He don't" are wrong, but sometimes we think they ain't. (Prochnow.)

51. The hardest part of living in the Ozarks is getting your kin folks to go back to the state they come from.

52. An Ozarker, while handing his wife over to the robber, was interrupted by the robber, who said, "Hold it pal...I said money or you life...NOT your wife!"

53. Did you hear about the hillbilly that rented an "Out House" from his neighbor and sub-rented the basement to his Yankee cousin from New Jersey?

54. A young man from the Ozark country, in Chicago for the first time, walked into an Automat and dropped several dollars' worth of nickels, dimes, and quarters into various coin-operated food dispensers and covered six tables with a wide variety of sandwiches, cakes, pies, salads, beverages, and puddings. Then he rushed gleefully to the cashier, changed more bills into silver, and began to put more coins into the slots and pulled out more dishes of food. The manager, who had been observing him, finally stopped him and demanded an explanation. "What's the matter?" the man said. "Are you sore at me because I'm winning?"

55. A Northerner got real thirsty traveling through the Ozarks and stopped at a farm house and ask for a drink. An old hillbilly woman, who had tobacco juice running down both sides of her mouth, came out, (At least it showed she was level headed.) She drew up a wooden bucket of water and handed him a gourd to drink from. He immediately thought, how many times has she drink out of that gourd with all of that tobacco juice? She was watching, so he thought where can he get on that gourd that she doesn't use. He went right down next to the handle and took a drink. She said, "That beats anything I've ever seen, City Feller. There's been a hundred men drink out of that dipper, but you are the only one that drinks out of it just like I do."

56. A Northerner was traveling endlessly through the rough Ozark mountains without seeing a soul for a long time. Finally he came to a remote post office that was flying the American flag. He quickly remarked to his companion, "Lord, it's good to know that we're still in the United States.

PEOPLE

Bald

1. I'm so bald that I stuck my head out the window the other day and got arrested for mooning.

2. I told my grandson that I traded my hair for brains. He said, "Grandpa, you sure got a raw deal."

3. My hair was once wavy, but now it's all beach.

4. The Lord just gave us each so many hormones. If you want to waste yours on hair, just go ahead.

5. You have to be bald to look mature, have to wear glasses to look distinguished, and have to have hemorrhoids to look concerned. And I've got all three of them.

6. I'm so bald that when I wash my forehead, I'm half bathed.

7. I would have parted my hair in the middle, but I have an uneven number of hairs.

8. There is one thing about baldness. It's neat.

9. I'm so bald I have to carry my dandruff in my pocket.

10. Baldness has it's advantages. When company comes, all you have to do is straighten your tie.

Little Boys

1. Two little boys were wandering along the beach, when one stopped to peek through a knothole into a bath house. "Who's in there – men or women?" his little friend asked. "I can't tell," the peeper replied, "they don't have any clothes on."

2. An 8-year-old boy asked his father: "Dad, would you punish me for something I didn't do?" "Of course not," said his father. "Fine," said the kid. "I didn't

do my homework."

3. Boy: "Can you write with your eyes closed?" Father: "Certainly." Boy: "Then sign my report card."

4. "Have you done your good deeds for the day?" a Scoutmaster asked three of his charges. "Yep," replied one, "we helped an old lady across the street." "So how come it took all three of you?" "She didn't want to go."

5. Small boy: I'm afraid of going to the hospital, mother. I'll be brave and take my medicine. But if I do have to go, I'm not going to let them palm off a baby on me like they did on you. I want a pup.

6. The whole family was gathered around the bus when little Johnny came home from his first day of kindergarten. Grandpa said, "How did you get along in school today?" "Fine: but I need to know how much is a million dollars for tomorrow." Grandpa was in a hurry so he just said, "Oh, that's a hell of a lot of money," and went on his way. The next evening when Johnny got off of the bus, Grandpa was there and ask him if he learned anything in school today. On that little Johnny kinda rubbed his fanny and said, "I learned one thing. The answer you gave me last night sure wasn't right."

7. The little boy wanted a red bicycle and he prayed for it daily. God told him to be good for six months and I'll give you a new a red bicycle. He said that he couldn't be good for that long. The boy kept trying to reduce God to three months, then two weeks with no results. Finally he saw the statue of Mary over on the dresser and he wrapped it up in a blanket and put it under the bed and said, "God if you ever want to see your mother again, you better get me that bicycle." (Rick Wheeler.)

8. "Mommy, where do people come from?" "Oh, from the dust of the earth." After a while the lad came back in and asked, "Where do they go when they die?" "Oh, they return to the dust of the earth." The little lad quickly said, "Well, mommy, you'd better go look under the bed, because somebody is either coming or going."

9. There was a lad who had the reputation of not being very bright. People had fun with him several times a day by placing a dime and a nickel on the open palm of his hand, and telling him to take his pick of the two. In each case the boy would take the nickel and then the crowd would laugh. A kind-hearted woman asked him one day if he didn't know the difference between a dime and a nickel, that a dime, though smaller, was worth more. "Sure, I know it," he replied, "but they wouldn't try me out on it any more if I took the dime."

10. A little boy sat with his arms crossed and a frown on his face when it was announced that his mother had given birth to a baby girl. What's the matter, his father asked? Aren't you happy about your new baby sister? Yeah, I guess, replied the tot, but there are a lot of things we needed more.

11. A little boy was attending his first wedding. After the service, his cousin asked him, "How many women can a man marry?" "Sixteen," the boy responded. His cousin was amazed that he knew the answer so quickly. "How did you know that?" "Easy," the little boy said. "All you have do to is add it up, like the preacher said: "Four better, four worse, four richer, four poorer."

12. "When is today tomorrow?" My five-year-old can't get. He asks me every morning, "Is it tomorrow yet?"

13. Heading home after a long, hot day of hiking, I was happy to see that a couple of the neighborhood boys had set up a juice stand. After handing over a quarter, I took a big drink out of my large plastic cup and turned to leave. Hey, sir, we need the cup back, one of the boys shouted. Planning to use it again? I asked. Yeah, he replied proudly. We've been using it all day.

14. Mother reprimanding her little son: "If you wanted to go fishing, why didn't you ask me first?" "Because, I wanted to go fishing."

15. I was very ugly as a kid. In fact I was kidnapped when I was young, and the kidnappers sent a note to my parents, "Either fork over $5,000, or you'll see him again."

16. I was so ugly that when I was born, the doctor slapped my mother.

17. I told my dad that I wanted a bubble bath. He complied. He brought the water to a boil.

18. I told my father that he never took me to the zoo. He said, "If they want you, they'll come and get you."

19. A kid was swimming in the pond. His dad said, "I told you not to swim in the pond." "I fell in." "If you fell in, how come your clothes are dry?" "I took them off. I had a hunch I might fall in."

20. "You have two sisters?" "yes." "What's their names?" "Hortense and Lassie." "Well, Lassie is a dog." "Wait 'til you see Hortense."

21. My dad taught me to be patriotic at a very early age. He laid on the stripes and I saw the stars.

22. Small boy to father. "I'm supposed to tell you there's going to be a small PTA meeting tomorrow night." "Small, do I have to go?" "Oh yes. It's just you, me, and the principal."

23. Do you think it will EVER get as cold as it did when dad was our age?

24. I found the best computer whiz to fix our system, but we need a note from his mother to get him out of day care.

25. A mother was scolding her little boy: "When that boy threw rocks at you, why didn't you tell me." "Why tell you? You couldn't hit the side of the barn."

26. Mommy, did the same stork that brought me also bring little bugs, mice, and lizards? The puzzled mother said, "I guess it was." "Then you really didn't do so bad after all, did you?"

27. Teacher to first grader; your paper is exactly the same as Joey's. Even the miss-spelled words are the same. Can you explain this? "Yes. We used the same pencil."

28. When you smell hickory smoke in the Ozarks, it usually indicates that somewhere a kid is getting a good whipping.

29. A little boy stuck his head in the door and said, "Mommy if I fell out of a tree, would you rather I'd tear my pants or break my leg?" "Why honey, I'd rather you'd tear your pants." "Well, you're going to be mighty happy, because that's exactly what I've done."

30. The teacher told the curious mother that her son was a very outstanding student. At least he is always put out standing in the halls.

31. One of the students spoke up and said, "He is in the office so much we thought he was an assistant principal."

32. A pat on the back develops character, if administered young enough and low enough.

33. Knock knock, who's there? Boo. Boo who? Oh, I'm sorry I made you cry.

34. Knock knock, who's there? Canoe. Canoe who? Canoe come out and play?

35. Knock knock, who's there? DuWayne. DuWayne who? Duwayne the bath tub, I'm drowning.

36. Any child can tell you that the sole purpose of having a middle name is so he can tell when he's really in trouble with his parents.

37. The kid was acting silly in class, and the teacher said, "Has anybody got his medicine?"

38. Mommy I'll be good for a nickel. What's the big idea? Why can't you be like your father and be good for nothing?

39. Sit down and tell Mommy a story. I can't sit down. I just told Daddy one.

40. Aunt to the little boy. The last time I saw you, you were only so high. The boy said, Yes, and you were only so wide.

41. "Daddy, are caterpillars good to eat?" "We don't discuss things like that at the dinner table." A short time later the boy said, "Never mind, dad. That caterpillar was on your lettuce, but he's all gone now."

42. A little boy came running in to the store. "My daddy is being chased by a bull." "What do you want me to do about it?" "Put some film in my camera."

43. A kid woke up at 1 a.m. and wanted his mother to tell him a story. She said, "Just wait 'till daddy comes home, and he'll tell us both one."

44. Salesman to little boy; "Is your mother home?" "Yes sir." The salesman kept knocking, but no body answered. "I thought you said your mother was home." "She is, but I don't live here."

45. The mother took little Irvin to kindergarten. She told the teacher that if he misbehaves, go back, but don't slap little Irvin. Slap the kid next to him, and that will scare little Irvin.

46. "Painless dentist, hah!" laughed little Tommy. "He's no different from any other dentist that I've seen!" "What do you mean?" asked his mother. Tommy smiled. "He screamed like crazy when I bit his finger."

47. Joe's son rushed in the door. "Dad! Dad!" he announced. "I got a part in the school play today!" " That's great, "Joe said proudly. "What part is it?" "I play the part of the father." Joe thought this over. "Go back tomorrow," he instructed, "and tell them you want a speaking role."

48. George Washington's father didn't punish him for cutting down the cherry tree, because George still had the hatchet in his hand.

49. Little Boy: "Why do cows eat grass?" Dad: "I don't know."
Little Boy: "Why do chickens lay eggs?" Dad: "I don't know."
Little Boy: "Why do birds fly?" Dad: "I don't know."
Little Boy: "Do you mind me asking you these questions, daddy?"
Dad: "Why no son, how else would you learn?"

50. Policewoman: "Why didn't you hang onto your mother's skirt?" Lost Child: "I couldn't reach it."

51. Two babies were in the hospital nursery discussing their place in the this new world they'd joined. One baby said, ''Are you a boy or a girl?'' "A boy." He

said. "How can you tell?" the other baby said. The baby said, "Just wait 'till that nurse leaves the room and I'll show you." She finally went out into the hall and the baby threw the covers back and said, "See, I'm a boy, I've got blue booties." (Darrell Peters.)

52. Teacher to first graders: "Children, today we are going to do something real unique. I want each of you to go to the blackboard and write your father's profession. "The first little boy got along very well. He wrote FARMER. The next boy wrote DOCTOR. Then James' dad was a sheet metal worker, and he wasn't quite sure how to spell it. He got up and wrote S-H-E, then he erased it and wrote S-H-I, then he erased it and wrote S-H-E again. The disgusted teacher said, "James, just go over to one side and we will continue while you're thinking. "OK, Freddy, you're next." He quickly said, "My daddy's a bookie, and I'm laying 9 to 5 odds that boy's going to write S...T on the blackboard."

Divorce

1. I started to get a divorce the other day, but got arrested for leaving the scene of an accident.

2. Do you know what a tornado, a termite and a divorce have in common? Somebody is going to loose a house.

3. The divorce lawyer asked the husband if this was true that he hadn't spoken a word to his wife in 20 years. He said, "Yes." "Why?"" "I didn't want to interrupt her."

4. The many times divorced blonde passed two men on the street, and one of them said, "There goes my ex-wife. Wonderful housekeeper." "She sure don't look like the type that would be a good housekeeper. Not at all." "Oh yes, she is though. Divorced three times and kept the house each time."

Little Girls

1. She's the picture of her father and the sound track of her mother.

2. Kids: "Have you children been good while I've been gone? "I Washed the dishes." "I wiped them dry." "What did you do (to the smallest on)? "I picked up the pieces."

3. To the baker's daughter: "Don't you sometimes feel tempted to eat a cupcake?" "Of course not, "that would be stealing. I only lick the icing off of them."

4. A small girl, enchanted with her new baby cousin, asked her mother, "Can't we have a baby?" "I don't believe so, darling," said her mother. "They cost too much." "How much?" inquired the child. "Oh, about $200," said the mother. The youngster thought a moment. "That's not very much when you consider how long one would last."

5. Dorothy, aged six, was watching her mother put cold cream on her face. "What's that for, Mommy?" she asked. "It's face cream, dear, to make me look beautiful." A little while later, after the cold cream had been wiped off, Dorothy looked at her mother for a minute, shook her head and remarked sadly, "Didn't

work, did it, Mommy?"

6. My 9 year old niece bought me perfume. "This is one of my favorites, I told her. How did you know what to buy?" "The man in the shop helped," she replied. "He did very well. Did he ask what I looked like, or what colors I like to wear, or how old I am?" "No," she answered. "He asked me how much money I had."

7. A mother and daughter were riding in a cab through New York City when the daughter noticed some scantily clad women loitering on a street corner. "Mommy," the little girl asked, "What are all those ladies doing?" "They're waiting for their husbands to come home from work," the mother replied. "C'mon, lady," the cabbie interjected, "Tell her the truth. They're hookers!" After a stunned silence, the daughter piped up, "Mommy, do hookers have children?" "Of course," the mother replied. "Where do you think cabbies come from?" (Dave Wagoner.)

Grandchildren

1. Tot to mom: Grandma and Grandpa are sure nice. How come they never had any kids?"

2. "Have I told you about my grandchildren?" "No, and I appreciate it."

3. As my wife boarded the bus, she asked the fellow in the first seat if he had any grandchildren. He said yes. So she asked the person in the second seat and he had some. She kept asking until she got to the back of the bus, and finally one old man didn't have any grandchildren. She said, "Good, I'll sit down and tell you about mine."

4. My 94-year-old grandma is here. She's with her parents.

5. "Oh grandma, there was a mouse swimming around in that bucket of milk that you just got from the cow." Did you take it out?" "No, I throwed the cat in."

6. My wife always hid the Easter Eggs where the grandkids could easily find them. But this year she put them out under the old setting hen. Well, the kids didn't find them, but when the old rooster came home, he jumped the fence and beat the devil out of the peacock.

7. At a pharmacy a woman asked if her friend could use the infant scales. They're out for repairs. Just hold the baby on the adult scales and weigh, then weigh the mother without the baby and subtract." "It won't work. I'm not the mother, I'm the grandmother."

8. My grand kid kept wanting me to make a noise like a frog. "Why are you always wanting me to make a noise like a frog?" "Cause grandma said that when you croaked, she would take us to Hawaii.

9. Grandma, enjoy your grandkids now because they think you're great. A couple of years from now and they won't think much of you." "How do you know that?" "Because I'm going to tell them."

10. I ran research all over the United States and when it was finished, I found out that I had the six best grandkids in the United States.

Indian

1. An American Indian sent the following message to the president: "Be careful with your immigration laws. We weren't with ours."

2. "When an American Indian film was shown recently at a theater in New York, two Indians were employed for advertising purposes and stationed in front of the theater. An inquisitive, jewel-bedecked woman haughtily asked one: "You're a real Indian, aren't you?" "Yes madam," was the courteous response. "How do you like our city?" she inquired. "Very fine, madam," replied the Indian. "How do you like our country?"

3. America is a great nation. When the white men discovered it, the Indians ran it. Then there were no taxes, no debt, and the women did all of the work – and we thought we could improve on that.

4. A history teacher asked her class why the Indians were the first people in North America. One boy popped up and said, "They had reservations."

Mother-In-Law

1. If you're ever tempted to commit bigamy, remember the penalty – two mothers-in-law.

2. "If you learned that the world would come to an end in six months, what would you do?" "I'd go stay with my mother-in-law." "Why that?" "Because it would be the longest six months of my life."

3. Mixed emotions is when you see your mother-in-law drive your new Cadillac over the cliff. You don't know whether to be happy or sad.

4. Behind every successful man stands a surprised mother-in-law.

5. The only animal he's afraid of is his mother-in-law. She's a bear.

6. The accident shocked the Ozark mountainside. A mule kicked a mother-in-law to death. A visitor said, "She must have been a wonderful woman, judging from such a large crowd at her funeral." The undertaker told him, "Men ain't here for the funeral, they're here to buy the mule."

7. My wife owes her beauty to me. She fell in a briar patch and scratched her face up so bad she had to have plastic surgery. They had to get the skin from me. I couldn't set down for weeks, but her face was as smooth as silk. She wanted to repay me, so I told her to just have her mother kiss her cheek.

8. Most mothers-in-law, are back-seat drivers; not mine, she sits on the hood.

9. As his good wife lay on her deathbed, she pleaded: "John, I want you to promise me that you'll ride in the same car with my mother at the funeral." "Okay, okay," he sighed, "but it's going to ruin my whole day."

10. Husband and wife were having a quarrel about their relatives. "You never have a single good word to say about any of my family," the husband shouted. "Oh yes I have," answered the wife. "To be perfectly honest, I like your mother-in-law better than mine."

Men

1. There's a lot of talk about Women's Lib, but when all is said and done, men still have the last word. It's "yes, dear."

2. I run things around this house. That's especially true when it comes to errands.

3. "Reincarnation: Does that mean I could come back as a worm or something?" Wife said, "No, you can't come back as the same thing."

4. "I can't go. I got to hurry home and explain to my wife." "Explain what?" "How do I know, I'm not home yet."

5. A man can be 100% stupid and never know it. A single man, that is.

6. "I won't be able to work today, my wife broke an arm." "But what does that have to do with your work?" "It was my arm she broke."

7. Man is not complete until he is married. Then he is finished.

8. I saw a man at the cemetery crying, "Why did you die, Oh why did you have to die?" "Is this man special to you sir?" "He's my wife's first husband."

9. Australian women prefer cats to men. What's the difference? Well, neither communicate. Both spend much time sleeping on the couch. Both stay out all night. The only difference is that cats don't miss the litter box.

10. On a crowded elevator, a man got real close to an attractive blonde. Suddenly the blonde wheeled and slapped him, and said, "If there's anything I can't stand, it's a pincher." After getting off of the elevator, the man and his wife were walking down the hall, and the man said to his wife, "That blonde is nuts. I didn't pinch her." His wife said, "Yes I know. I did."

11. "Do you know that young couple that moved in down the street? They must be lovely people. Every morning when he leaves for work, they stand in the doorway and kiss and hug so endearingly. On the way to the car they keep waving and throwing kisses." "Why don't you do that?" "I barely know the woman."

12. You think I'm a fool? I was born at night, but not last night.

13. Did you ever hear someone say, "I'd hate to be him." "Well, I'm him."

14. One of those 'possums you were hunting last night left his lipstick in the truck.

15. What's the matter, Joe? You look terrible. I've got seenus. Don't you mean Sinus, No. I mean seenus. I was out with a married woman last night, and her husband seen us.

16. Frank irritated friends with his optimism. Friends improvised a story just to test Frank. They told him that Jim came home and found his wife in bed with another man and he shot the man. Frank said, "It could have been worse." "How?" "If it had of been the day before, I'd be dead."

17. A creative request for time off: "My wife wants to get pregnant tonight, and I'd like to be there when it happens."

18. Who is the richest, the man with seven million dollars, or the man with seven kids? The man with seven kids is richer. The man with seven million wants more.

19. I once knew a man who only opened his mouth to change feet.

20. I cannot indulge in such sports as water skiing, mountain climbing, and water polo, because of my bad back. It has a yellow streak running up it.

21. He wasn't from the Ozarks because he had hair and teeth.

22. "You say that you're name is Chow mein and you were a Japanese kamikaze pilot in World War II? How could that be? You would have gone on a suicide mission and be dead? "My name is Chicken Chow Mein."

23. That IRS man is his own worst enemy. The Ozarker spoke up and said, "Not while I'm alive, he isn't."

24. A lady offered John Wesley a suggestion. "Your bow tie is too conspicuous and offers too much pride." "OK lady, fix it with the scissors as you like. Now can I offer you a suggestion?" "Yes," He took the scissors and said, "Now stick out your tongue."

25. He is not as smart as God, but he is as smart as God was when God was his age.

26. "Did I bring your lawnmower back last month?" "No." "Now, what'll I do? I wanted to borrow it again."

27. An Ozarker to his uncle, "How come your feet are so big?" "I grew up and went barefooted in the rich soil of the midwestern plains." "Uncle Jim, you must have done a lot of sitting in that rich soil too."

28. "See here young man, who told you to plant all that shrubbery in my front yard?" "Why, your wife, of course." "Mighty pretty, isn't it?"

29. "I want some fire insurance." "Ok, what's your address?" "Not on my home. I want it on me, because every time I get a job, I get fired."

30. In 7 days God created earth and man. On the 8th day He created Ozarkers.

31. "If you were locked in a room with Mohamr Quadfi, Sadamn Hussein, and your IRS agent, and had a gun and only two bullets, what would you do?" "I'd shoot the IRS agent twice."

32. "Do you jog like everyone is doing these days?" "Nah, I get enough exercise just being pallbearer for those who do jog."

33. "What kind of a fellow is Tom?" "I don't believe I've met him." "Well, if you see two fellows talking anywhere, and one of them looks bored to death, the other one is bound to be Tom."

34. I play the guitar and the French Harp. No one is brave enough to tell me to stop.

35. It seems like I've been married since I was four years old.

36. An Ozark Hillbilly shot his wife in the arms of another. The jury verdict was justifiable homicide. As he was leaving the courtroom, the judge asked him, why he shot his wife and not the lover. He said, "Better to shoot a woman once, than a different man each night."

37. "A $75 hotel bill???" "Yes, $40 for room, $35 for meals." "But I didn't eat here. "They were here for you. If you didn't eat them, it's your fault. "Then I'll charge you $35 for kissing my wife." "But I didn't kiss your wife." "She was here for you. If you didn't kiss her, that's your fault."

38. H. Roe Bartle, mayor of K.C. and a large person weighing 270 pounds, saw an unusual set of scales at the airport. A little girl stepped on it and it said, "44 pounds please." A lady stepped on it and it said, "120 pounds please." So he stepped

on and it said, "One at a time please."

39. D T. Chamberlain and I would always trade stories at meetings. Every time I would tell one that would make him laugh, he would say, "Same Old Bob." Every time it wouldn't be any different, "Same Old Bob." So at the last meeting, he abbreviated it. He just simply said, "SOB."

40. Old drug pushers never die, they just go to pot.

41. An Ozarker commenting on a banker that wouldn't loan him any money: "They must of weaned him when the sign was wrong."

42. My wife, who has a talent for do-it-yourself projects, was laying tile in the kitchen while I relaxed in the living room. A friend stopped by and said, sarcastically, "You don't know how to do anything, do you?" "I can do one thing," I replied. "I know how to pick a woman."

43. I asked to borrow a wheelbarrow from a neighbor. He said that he had loaned it to his son. I told him that my grandfather always told me never to loan anything to your kid, because you will never get it back. To that he responded, "Well, it's not even my wheelbarrow. It's my dad's."

44. I have a gorgeous new secretary and my wife asked me how much I pay her. I said, "$75." Fortunately, she didn't ask me how often.

45. I happen to know that my competitor's secretary loves to go to the race track and sit in front of the starting gate. It's the only chance she gets to see a horse's front!

46. BUSY – A go getter is sorry he got her. (Prochnow.)

47. A gentleman is one who never swears at his wife while ladies are present. (Anon.)

48. Before criticizing your wife's faults, remember that they may have prevented her from getting a better husband. (Prochnow.)

49. If my son would talk back to me, I'd slap him. One time he said, "I'm not going to school today, because the kids don't like me and the teachers don't like me." His mother said, "Son, you are going to school, because you're 40 years old and you're the principal."

50. She wants to have a natural child birth, and her husband doesn't. So he has been going to those classes by himself.

51. My wife is on a diet...She told me she was losing 4 pounds a week...If my figures are correct, I'll be completely rid of her in 15 months.

52. The executive's wife picked up their little daughter and asked, "Do you like your new nurse, dear?" "No, I don't," the girl replied. "I hate her. I'd like to grab her and bite her neck like daddy does."

53. John had a big time with the boys one night and before he realized it, the next day had dawned. He hesitated to call home, until a bright thought hit him. He phoned his wife, and when she answered, he shouted, "Don't pay the ransom honey, I escaped."

54. A (staid) gentleman was upset at the dress of some young people on the street. "Just look at that one," he barked to a bystander, "is it a boy or a girl?" "It's a girl. She's my daughter." "Oh forgive me, madam," apologized the gentleman, "I didn't know you were her mother." "I'm not," snapped the bystander, "I'm her father."

55. A man had been talking for hours about himself and his achievements. "I'm a self-made man, that's what I am - a self - made man," he said. "You've knocked off work too soon," came a quiet voice from the rear.

56. My wife will outlive me, no doubt about it. You know why women live longer that men? Simple, they're not married to women.

57. Not going to get a birthday present for my wife this year. She hasn't used what I got her last year yet!" "What did you get her last year?" "A cemetery plot."

58. Many a man has tried to pull the wool over his wife's eyes by using the wrong yarn.

59. My goal was to retire at 30. I did. I had enough money to last me 30 days.

60. The man appeared at the newspaper office to place a classified ad offering $200 for the return of his wife's cat. "That's a high price for a cat," said the editor. "Not for this one," replied the man. "I've already drowned it."

61. Where do forest rangers go to "get away from it all?"

62. A man went to the local barber for a shave. After being cut several times, he asked, "Hey, buddy, do you have an extra razor?" the barber responded, " C e r - tainly. Do you want to shave yourself?" "No", he answered. "I thought I might be able to defend myself."

63. Adam and Eve: After a few days, the Lord called to Adam and said, It's time for you and Eve to begin the process of populating the earth so I want you to kiss her. Adam answered, "Yes Lord, but what is a kiss?" So the Lord gave a brief description to Adam, who took Eve by the hand and took her to a nearby bush....A few minutes later, Adam emerged and said, "Thank you Lord, that was enjoyable." And the Lord replied, "Yes Adam, I thought you might enjoy that and now I'd like you to caress Eve." And Adam said, "What is a "caress?" So the Lord again gave Adam a brief description and Adam went behind the bush with Eve. Quite a few minutes later, Adam returned, smiling, and said, "Lord, that was even better than the kiss." And the Lord said, "You've done well, Adam. And now I want you to make love to Eve." And Adam asked, "What is 'make love' Lord?" So the Lord again gave Adam directions and Adam went again to Eve behind the bush, but this time he reappeared in two seconds. And Adam said, "Lord, what is a 'headache'?"

64. Does This Describe Your Husband?

Q: What do you call a man with half a brain?
A: Gifted.
Q: How many men does it take to change a roll of toilet paper?
A: We don't know; it has never happened.
Q: Why are blonde jokes so short?
A: So men can remember them.
Q: What is the difference between men and government bonds?
A: The bonds mature...eventually.
Q: What makes men chase women who they have no intention of marrying?
A: The same instinct which makes dogs chase cars they have no intention of driving.
Q: Why don't men have a midlife crisis?
A: They're stuck in adolescence.
(Frank Martin III.)

Old

1. I'm so old that when I was born the Dead Sea wasn't even sick.

2. I'm so old that when I was born they're were only 13 colonies.

3. I'm so old I've got an autographed copy of the Bible.

4. I'm so old I went to a nude beach the other day and had to park in the handicapped section.

5. I'm so old they've discontinued my blood type.

6. I'm so old that to me the daily double is prune juice and an enema.

7. An 80-year-old man was getting married. "Why do you want to get married at your age?" "It isn't that I want to. I have to."

8. A grandmother dated an 80-year-old man. Had to slap him three times. "You mean he actually got fresh with you?" "No. I thought he was dead"

9. You're celebrating your 50th wedding anniversary? Is that all in a row?

10. Every day above ground is a good one.

11. What doesn't hurt, doesn't work. And when you sink your teeth in a steak, they stay there.

12. If you are yearning for the good old days, just turn off the air conditioner.

13. At 16 you think you will live forever, at 60 you wonder how you've lasted so long.

14. The older your generation gets, the wilder the younger generation becomes.

15. The trouble is that the young don't know what to do, and the old can't do what they know to do.

16. In youth, everything matters too much; in old age nothing matters much.

17. Old age sure isn't for sissies.

18. Andy Williams said that he went to visit a friend in the nursing home and had to sit outside his room on a bench for a while. A nurse came by and asked, "who are you and can I help you?" "Don't you know who I am?" "No, but if you will step to the desk and give them your number, they can tell you who you are."

19. Three old Ozark men at an Old Folks Home were discussing the ideal way of dying. The first, age 74, said he'd like to crash in a car going 100 miles per hour. The second, age 87, said he'd like to take his finish in a jet plane going 900 miles per hour. The third, age 95, said, "I'd like to be shot by a jealous husband."

20. A man, after falling down a flight of stairs, asked his landlord why he didn't light up his dark hallway. The landlord replied, "I had a light there for three years. No one fell, so I took it away."

21. Old Uncle Jed died happy at a hunnert and four. In fact it was zackly hunnert degrees the day he died.

22. Went to a gay nineties party the other night; the men were gay and the women were ninety.

23. Satchel Page said, "How old would you be if you didn't know how old you was?"

Personal

1. I bought some scented toilet paper and I asked the merchant, "When are you supposed to smell of that." (Yakoff.)

2. I bought some diapers that you only change once per week. You've seen them advertised in the store, "Holds up to 18 Pounds." (Yakoff.)

3. If a mute swears, does his mother wash his hands with soap?

4. He is a high-tech ventriloquist. He can throw his voice mail.

Teenagers

1. Too many parents tie up their dogs and let their 16 year olds run loose.

2. I am not young enough to know everything. (James M. Barrie.)

3. You're never too old to learn...unless, of course, you're a teenager.

4. The old believe everything; the middle-aged suspect everything; the young know everything. (Oscar Wilde.)

5. A sure sign of teenage years is when your children stop asking you where they came from and start refusing to tell you where they're going .

6. How come it takes so little time for a child who is afraid of the dark to become a teenager who wants to stay out all night?

7. "It isn't a very good picture of him. It doesn't show his convertible."

8. "That new boy next door gave me his class ring. What do you do when you love the ring but can't stand the boy?"

9. "Where did you get that shiner?" "My girlfriend gave it to me" But I thought she was out of town! "That's what I thought too."

10. Remember, it's the fresh egg that gets slapped in the pan.

11. The Ozarker to his girlfriend; "I didn't hardly recognize you since you had your warts burned off."

12. She's the picture of her father and the sound track of her mother.

13. I want to borrow the car dad!" "OK, if you will cut that long hair." "The Bible says that Jesus had long hair." "Yes, and he walked every-where he went."

14. A boy is grown up when he walks around a puddle. (Prochnow.)

15. Many a boy at sixteen can't believe that some day he will be as dumb as his dad. (Prochnow.)

16. I was adopted, but they brought me back.

17. My brother is a fast dresser. Once he did it in two minutes flat. That's pretty good too, considering that he was hiding under the bed at the time.

18. A math teacher died and had saved little, barely enough to cover the doctor and hospital, with nothing for burial. The board members solicited funds for her burial until they were just down to one dollar. They were so desperate that they approached a kid who was a total stranger. Could you give me one dollar to bury a math teacher. "Why yes. Here's five dollars. Go bury five of them."

19. Undoubtedly the peak mental period is between the ages of four an 18. At four, we have all of the questions. At 18, we know all the answers.

20. Sure you can use the car...once you've demonstrated your ability to use the power mower.

21. It costs more to amuse a child now-a-days than it did to educate his father.

22. Few things are more satisfying than seeing your children have teenagers of their own.

23. Two mothers were discussing the problems of teenagers. One woman asked, "Is your son hard to get out of bed in the morning?" "No," replied the other. "I just open the door and throw the cat on his bed." "How does that wake him?" "The dog sleeps at the foot of the bed."

24. It was a bright spring morning and four high school boys decided to skip classes. Arriving after lunch, they explained to the teacher that their car had a flat tire along the way. To their relief, the teacher smiled understandingly, and said: "You boys missed a test this morning. Please take seats apart from one another and get out your paper and pencil." When the boys were seated, she continued, "Answer this question: Which tire was flat?"

25. The young Romeo helped his date into the car and said, "I like to take an experienced girl home." "I am not an experienced girl," she declared. " T h a t may be," he replied, "but you're not home yet, either."

Teenagers Dating

1. A 16-year-old girl hollered, "Oh, look. There's the car my friend Lorie has been dating."

2. Her heart belongs to me, but the rest of her kept going out with other guys.

3. A schoolmate ran away with my best friend. Now I have no dog.

4. John, let's not look for a girl at this dance any longer. If you'd run a bunch of quail through there, they'd all point."

5. My last girl friend left me for a tractor salesman. Didn't even let me know – I just got a John Deere letter.

6. He's like a Don Juan to the ladies, they Don Juan any-thing to do with him.

7. "Can I come in?" "No." I never ask a man in on the first date." How about the last date."

8. Scientists say kissing started because of a craving for salt. They say a caveman discovered he could cool off on a hot day by licking his neighbor's cheek. Then he found it was more fun if his neighbor was female. Then he forgot all about the salt.

9. An Ozarker watching a real good looking, shaply blonde crossing the street said, "Nature has been real good to her."

10. A young couple went to the Justice of the Peace to get married. He said he didn't marry on Sunday. The disappointed boy then turned to him and calmly said, "Could you just say a few words to tie us over the weekend?"

11. A boy arrived in a neighboring town about 30 minutes early to pick up a

blind date, so he went by a candy store. He ordered a large, a medium and a small box of candy. The manager ask why three boxes. The boy said he had a date in town and if it was real bad, he'd give her the small box, if it was fairly good, he'd give her the medium one. If it was an extra good one, he'd give her the big one. At meal time the father walked in as they sat down to the table. The father said the boy could ask the blessing. The boy prayed for 15 minutes. That evening on the porch swing the girl said to the boy, "I didn't realize that you were that spiritual." The boy said, "And I didn't realize your dad ran a candy store, either."

Engagements

1. "Will you marry me?" The pretty lady replied, "If you really loved me, you wouldn't even ask me to do that."

2. Dear Ann Landers: "Should I tell my fiancee I wear false teeth?" She replied, "Just marry him and keep your mouth shut."

3. The girl said, "I won't marry him, mother. He's an atheist and he don't believe in hell." The mother said, "Marry him and we'll prove it."

4. My fiance said, "Will you make a date for our wedding?" "You mean you can take a date to your own wedding?" (Yakoff.)

5. Before the wedding Linda wanted to have a shower. That was a good idea right there. (Yakoff.)

Wedding

1. "Do you, Jud Smith," intoned the mountain minister, "take this woman fer bet'r-worse, in sickness er health, good times er bad, sunshine er sor...." "Doggit, Parson," interrupted the bride, "stop tryin t' scare him out!"

2. Preacher to groom at a wedding ceremony, "It's I do, young man, not what ever."

3. "If anyone knows why these two should not be wed, let him speak now or forever hold his peace," said the clergyman. "I'd like to say something," piped up a nervous voice. "You keep out of this," said the clergyman, "You're the groom."

4. After the hillbilly wedding, a local resident shuffled up to the bride's father. Commenting on the somewhat reluctant appearance of the groom, he said: "Say, Zeke, your new son-in-law poked up to the altar as though he had lead in his pants." Zeke shifted his chew of tobacco and grunted: "He did."

5. A shotgun wedding: "A matter of wife or death.

Newlyweds

1. Guest at wedding reception: "Are you the bridegroom?" Young man: "No ma'am, I was eliminated in the semifinals."

2. A newly married man asked his wife, "Would you have married me if my father hadn't left me a fortune?" "Honey," the woman replied sweetly, "I'd have

married you no matter who left you a fortune."

3. The trouble was, I went into marriage with both eyes closed – her father closed one and her brother closed the other. (Max Karffmann)

4. Bride: "When we go into the lobby, lets try and make other people believe we've been married a long time." Groom: "That's okay with me, but do you think you can carry both suitcases?"

5. Realtor, to young couple: The only house I have in your price range is now occupied by a family of blue jays.

6. He's the kind of a fellow that turns the lights out on his wedding night and will be in bed before the room gets dark.

7. The new bride and groom were canoeing on a small lake when a violent storm struck. As the wind howled and the waves rose, the young groom prayed: "If only we get out of this, I'll give up smoking...I'll give up drinking....I'll give...." Just then the bride interrupted: "Don't give up everything, George. Paddle!"

8. First Neighbor: "I wonder if his bride is a good housekeeper?" Second Neighbor. "I'm afraid not. The day I dropped in she was trying to open an egg with a can opener."

9. "The two things I cook best," said the newly married bride, "are meat loaf and peach cobbler." As he looked at the plate before him, the young groom asked, "And which is this?"

10. Grandpa was going on his honeymoon. They left Willow Springs, Mo. headed for West Plains, Mo. On the way down, he put his hand on her knee. She said, "We're married now. You can go a little farther if you want to." So he drove clear on to Hardy, Arkansas.

11. A hillbilly who hadn't been married very long came home one day and found his wife bending over the tub, washing clothes. He grabbed her and kissed the back of her neck. A moment later he gave her a hard punch in the ribs. "What's the big idea?" cried his wife, her eyes flashing with anger. "That," shouted her husband, "is for not turning around to see who it was!"

Marriage

1. When a man and a woman get married, they become one. Our only trouble was, we could never decide which one.

2. Marriage is a bargain. And somebody has to get the worst of a bargain. (Helen Rowland.)

3. All men are born free and equal but many of them grow up and get married. (Prochnow.)

4. Marriage is just like sitting in a bathtub. Once you get used to it, it's not so hot.

5. I didn't know I had so many problems until I got married. Then I was sure glad she was there to point them out to me.

6. To an applicant for a job. "Can you pick lemons?" "You bet I can. I've been married five times."

7. If you were my husband, I'd put poison in your food. If I was your husband, I'd eat it. (Winston Churchill and Lady Astor.)

8. The best thing about marriage is that you don't have to date anymore. (At least it's frowned upon.)

9. Do you think my husband will love me when my hair turns gray? "He should, he's already loved you through four or five different colors."

10. It's been 45 years of marriage. It's been that long since anything I said mattered.

11. It matters little who wears the pants in the family just as long as there's money in the pockets.

12. Everything is compromise, compromise. Like I wanted to have a bachelor party. She didn't. So we compromised – I didn't have one.

13. "Let's eat at the steak house, or we could eat at the Chinese place." "But I hate Chinese food!" "No you don't. Right, right, right, I forgot. I love Chinese food."

14. Let's see now. What is it that I hate. Oh yah, it's football.

15. I'm learning though. Until I was married, I never realized what a crappy driver I was.

16. A fellow killed his wife after 20 years of marriage. Probably the first decision he made since his wedding.

17. The way I got married is that I ran an ad in the paper. It read, "A 21-year-old man wants to marry a 20-year-old girl who drives a tractor. Please send picture of tractor."

18. How did I actually find my wife? Well, a bunch of us Ozark country boys heard that someone was bringing a wagonload of girls to town from way back in the hills. When they got there with them, I just picked the ticks off of one of them and she followed me home.

19. Herb James said the way he got his wife was that his dad said to him that as old as he was he should be getting married, but be sure and get a good worker. He was then driving by a cornfield and saw a girl hoeing corn. At that he just stopped and asked her if she wanted to get married. She said, "Yes." So he said, "O.K., just come along with me. My dad wanted me to get a good 'hoer.'"

20. One of my mother's favorite stories was that when dad asked her to marry him and live on a farm, she said, "Well I can do about anything on a farm but work in the garden, because I'm no 'Hoer.'"

21. Henry had 12 kids. He robbed the cradle when he got married, and he felt so guilty that he's been all of these years trying to fill it back up.

22. To get to his house, go down a long lane. You'll see one kid, then another and another and etc. There will be a duck sitting in the yard. Well, actually that isn't a duck. It's a stork with it's legs worn off.

23. My wife won a trip to Las Vegas for two. She went twice.

24. My wife and I have words, but I never get to use mine.

25. I know my wife is an Angel, because she's always up in the air.

26. My wife and I were traveling through the Ozarks and got into a big argument. We didn't speak for probably an hour. We passed by a pasture that had a mule in it, and I said to her, "Is that some of your relation?" She said, "By marriage."

27. My cousin was visiting from California and he was on his fourth wife. I

asked him what happened to them, and he said that the first one died of eating poison mushrooms. The second one died of eating poison mushrooms. What happened to the third one? She died of a severe blow on the head. What caused the blow on the head? She wouldn't eat the mushrooms.

28. An unhappy looking young man entered the register's office. "Are you sure," he asked, "that was a marriage license you sold me last year?" "Of course. Why do you ask?" "Because I've led a dog's life ever since .

29. The only thing worse than a bachelor is the bachelor's son.

30. A dress manufacturer called on his physician. "I'm an absolute wreck," he explained. "I'm nervous, tense, and I can't sleep." "That's because you insist upon taking your troubles to bed with you," the physician pointed out. "Who can avoid it?" the patient asked. "My wife refuses to sleep alone."

31. Marriage is wonderful. It is great to have someone to greet you with a big kiss and hug and a kind word. If they do, you're in the wrong house.

32. Teacher explaining to the class that bigamy means having two wives at one time. "Now, can anyone here tell me what word means having only one wife?" "I can teacher – monotony."

33. There is nothing like the joy of parenthood, especially when all the children are in bed.

34. The phone rang and the Ozarker rushed out of bed to answer it. "I'm sorry, you'll have to call the weather bureau for that information," he said. "Who says that, dear?" his wife asked. "Oh, just some guy who wanted to know if the coast was clear."

35. The meek Ozark husband finally decided to be boss. He shook his fist and growled at his wife, "From now on, you do as I say. I want supper right now, then get upstairs and lay out my clothes. And do you know who's going to dress me in my tuxedo?" "I sure do," she screamed. "The undertaker."

36. An Ozarker was trying to make out with a good looking girl, and he told her that he was going to inherit all of his grandpa's money, and that he was real rich. So she married grandpa.

Wife

1. "Do you ever wake up grumpy?" "No, I usually let her sleep."

2. The Ozarker's wife told him to remind her to put a steak on his black eye when we get home. He said, "I ain't got no black eye." "Wait 'til we get home."

3. My wife and I had a big argument. I asked her how would she like it if I didn't see her for about three days? She said that will be just fine. And I didn't see her the first day, I didn't see her the second day or the third day; on the fourth day I could see her just a little bit out of one eye.

4. I'm going to be buried in a Wal-Mart parking lot. That way my wife will come by to see me three times a week.

5. The wife said, "Honey, I have good news and bad news." "Oh, give me the good news. After such a terrible day at the office, I can't stand any bad news." "Well, the air bags sure work well in your new Lincoln Continental." (Rick Wheeler.)

6. My wife has a great personality, but not for human beings.

7."Did you ever look at a woman and wish you were single?" "Yeah, My wife."

8. Man becomes the head of the family. (Yeah, right). No one told me that the woman becomes the neck of the family. She'll turn the head any where she wants. Why do you think we call them a pain in the neck? (Yakoff Smirnoff.)

9. I met an old friend I hadn't seen in years. "Tell me about your wife," I said. "Has she kept her figure?" "Kept it?" he repeated. "She's doubled it."

10. My wife reminded me that Aunt Martha pays our rent, mother buys us food, sister sends us clothes. She said, "I wish we could do better." I said, "You ought to. You got two uncles that don't send us a dime."

11. Wife: "If it weren't for my money, this television set wouldn't be here. If it weren't for my money, the chair you're sitting in wouldn't be here. If it weren't for my money, this house wouldn't be here." Husband: "And if it weren't for your money, I wouldn't be here."

12. My wife should have been a lawyer, because everything I say she turns into an argument. We've been holding hands every since we've been married. If we would ever let go, we'd kill each other.

13. "My wife is like an old shoe." "You mean comfortable?" "No. All worn out but her tongue."

14. "My wife's just like she was when we got married." "You mean your wife still looks like a bride after 25 years?" "No, she still cooks like a bride."

15. Took her to a beautician and they put a mud pack on her. She was real pretty for about three weeks until the mud fell off.

16. Go ahead women. Put on the powder and paint. I say if the Old Red Barn needs a coat of paint, you'd better give it one.

17. The trouble with all that makeup though, it begins to defrost about 9 o'clock.

18. "I saw your wife downtown today. She really had a hard time parking the car between two trucks." "Did she make it?" "Yes." "Then it wasn't my wife."

19. A man can tell what kind of a time he's having at a party by simply looking at his wife.

20. He's smarter than I am. He could have married my wife and didn't.

21. I'd rather take my wife along than to kiss her goodbye.

22. I quit the national auction business, because every time I would leave home I'd kiss the wife goodbye and say, "Goodbye Mother of Four." Then one time when I kissed her goodbye she said, "Good By father of three"

23. She ate so much substitute that she has Artificial Diabetes. (Pat Cash.)

24. One man says he would like to go back to the days when his wife's meals were carefully thought out instead of carefully thawed out.

25. My wife was too beautiful for words – but not for arguments. (John Barrymore.)

26. When I lost my wife every family in town offered me another; but when I lost my horse, no one offered to make him good.

27. I like that one about the henpecked meteorologist who says his wife speaks at 150 words a minute, with gusts up to 180.

28. The wife is always asking for money; $200, $75, $50. What does she do with it? Don't know, I never give her any.

29. "The wife and I made an agreement never to go to bed angry. "You mean

you never go to bed angry?" "No, but I haven't slept in ten days."

30. My wife stopped me from biting my nails. She hid my teeth.

31. I discovered a way to make the wife drive more carefully. If she has an accident, the paper will print her age.

32. My wife says to make me happy, all she needs to know is how to act like a lady, think like a man, and work like a dog.

33. The wife took a speed-reading course. Now she gets out of the bath room in half of the time.

34. She's so mean that she reminds me of my wife when I'm overdrawn at the bank.

35. Man went to the doctor and after the examination, the doctor called the wife in to talk separately. He said stress is killing him. It must be corrected or he'll soon be dead. Your husband must have breakfast in bed, his favorite chair and TV program, the best of food, and you must take him to shows and treat him gently with much affection. Going home, the husband ask the wife what the doctor said. "He said, you're going to die." (Rick Wheeler.)

36. Do you ever consider divorce? Divorce, No. Murder, Yes.

37. Everytime I come home with my mind made up to stay home, she has her face made up to go out!

38. Tom: "Your wife used to be so nervous. Now she seems quite cured." John: "She is. The doctor told her nervousness was a sign of old age."

39. Was going to ride a helicopter. The pilot ask our weight. My wife quickly got off. "Aren't you going dear?" "No. If everyone is lying as much about their weight as I am, this thing won't fly."

40. A neighbor said that you were sure the boss. He said that he passed by the other night and saw your wife on her hands and knees just screaming and begging and carrying on. She was really begging. "Yeah, she was saying, "(You coward, come out from under that bed.)"

41 . The lodge member approached Henry to "put the bite on him." We're having a raffle for a poor widow," he told Henry. "Will you buy a ticket?" "Nope," Henry retorted. "My wife wouldn't let me keep her if I won."

42. The wife of a corporation president presented him with a bottle of shampoo. "What's this for?" the executive asked. "Oh, it's not for you," his wife said. "It's for your secretary. She seems to be losing her blonde hair all over your suits."

43. Two guys were chatting at a cocktail party. "Your wife certainly brightens the room," one said to the other. "Her mere presence is electrifying. "It ought to be, "the other man replied. ""Everything she's wearing is charged."

44. He told the boys at the coffee shop that next week is our 50th wedding anniversary. He told them that he took his wife to South America for their 25th anniversary. ''Oh, my that was great. What are you going to do for the 50th one?" "I'm thinking about going back down there and picking her up."

Women

1. God made man and earth then rested. Then he made woman and nobody's rested since.

2. Give a woman an inch and she thinks she is a ruler.

3. I never knew what happiness was until I got married. Then it was too late.

4. There will be no women in Heaven. Why? Revelations 8:1 says there is going to be 30 minutes of silence there.

5. It's real easy to get women to listen to you. Just whisper everything.

6. Adam was created first in order to give him a chance to say something.

7. Men like the simple things of life–women.

8. Even in the stone age, when women wrote down their ages, they were chiseling.

9. That lady over there has something that will knock your eye out: A husband about six-foot-four.

10. Two women heading home from shopping, one of them called out to the other, "I'll call you when I get home." Then a moment later, she shouted, "Better yet, you call me. You'll get home before I will."

11. "You look mighty nice." "Thank you, I wish I could say the same about you." "You could if you was as big a liar as me."

12. Since an overcrowded planet, seems in store for the human race, it's great that using elastic, helps women take one third less space.

13. "Please punch that button on the dash there." "What's it for?" "That 's to engage the warning signal – that we have a "women driver aboard."

14. "How much is the fare?" "The taxi driver said, "There is no charge lady. After all, you did most of the driving."

15. Helen told Martha that you told her what I told you not to tell her, but don't tell her that I told you she told me what I told you not to tell her.

16. She has buried four husbands. Two of them were just napping.

17. Woman shot her husbands at close range. How could you tell? Powder marks on his face. Yessir, that's why she shot him.

18. Ever see a perfect woman?" "Heard of one." "Who?" "My husband's first wife."

19. Triplets – I just can't imagine it. "Yes, and the doctor says it only happens once in every 200,000 times." "Once in every 200,000 times!!" How do you ever find time to do your house work?"

20. Standing in a checkout line, I was joshing with a tourist in line in front of me. Pretty soon she had enough of our Ozark humor and she said, "Look here mister, if you don't stop harassing me, I'll write a check."

21. "God" I want to ask two questions. Why are women so soft and pretty? "So you'd be attracted to them!" "Why are they so dumb?" "So they'd be attracted to you."

22. To a second grader – Describe a set of scales. All I know is that you stand on it and it makes you mad.

23. "My mommy can talk an hour on any subject." "So what. My mommy can talk an hour without a subject."

24. There may be something to reincarnation. Some women of 35 can remember things that happened 45 years ago.

25. My daddy can beat your daddy. Big deal, so can my mommy.

26. There is an old Japanese proverb that says: When women subtract years from their age, the years are not lost. They are merely added to the ages of her women friends.

27. I wouldn't mind hearing about her operation, if she'd only stop and listen to mine.

28. What's my age? I'm approaching 50. I'm just coming at it from the other side.

29. Never send a boy to do a man's job send a woman.

30. The best man for a job is often a woman.

31. Do you know why the brains of a woman are the size of a pea? Cause they're swollen.

32. BARGAIN – A woman will buy anything she thinks the store is losing money on. (Kin Hubbard.)

33. BARGAIN – Women will buy anything that's one to a customer. (Lewis.)

34. Women's right to vote–giving a woman a ballot won't amount to much, for none of them would admit that they are old enough to vote until they were too old to take any interest in politics.

35. Don't ever give a woman advice. Never give a woman anything she can't wear in the evening.

36. The wife who drives from the back seat is no worse than the husband who cooks from the dinner table.

37. In the Ozarks, if you are dressing up, it means that you got to put on some clothes.

38. At a checkout stand a woman had a remote control in her purse."Why do you carry that remote with you?" "Because my husband wouldn't come shopping with me, and I just thought that this was the worst punishment I could do to him."

39. Doctor couldn't find anything wrong with her, so I'll just have to ask some questions. "Do you eat regular?" Three meals a day. Do you sleep regular? Go to bed at 9 pm, and sleep 8 hours every night. Do you go to the bathroom regularly? "Every night at 9 pm just before going to bed." "Well, the only thing I can think of is to give you a shot of penicillin." There were three little germs inside hearing all of this, and the thoughts of penicillin just infuriates them. They begin to bustle around and one of them said, "What are you going to do? I'm going to hole up in that trap in the esophagus that lets the aspirin and things go by. "What are you going to do? I'm going to hide in the appendix." The third one said, "You two do what you want to, but I'm taking that 9 o'clock out of here."

40. ANTI-FREEZE-The quickest way to make your own anti-freeze is to hide her nightie. (Anon.)

41. Three dumb blondes were stranded on an island and they prayed all night to get back to the mainland. At daybreak God granted them one wish each. The first asked for the strength to get back, and she was granted the strength to swim back. The second asked for the wisdom to get back and was granted the knowledge to cut down a tree to make a canoe and row back to the mainland. The

third asked for even more wisdom than the other two, so she was turned in to a man and she just went over to the bridge and walked across.

42. A neighbor lady won $15,000 in Reno, and she got so excited that she said she wet her pants. She said that it could have been worse though; she could have won $20,000.

43. If exercise eliminates fat, how come woman get double chins?

44. Aunt Lucy was walking down a dimly lit street when a holdup man jumped out on the bushes. "Give me your money," he demanded. "I don't have any," she replied. He proceeded to search her thoroughly. "I guess you were telling me the truth," he muttered angrily. "You don't have any money on you." For Goodness Sake," she said, "Don't stop looking. I can write you a check."

45. The woman entered the hardware store and asked for a three- quarter-inch plug. "A male plug, female plug, or both?" she was asked. With great patience, she replied, "I just want to stop a leak...I'm not going to breed them."

46. They're building a lot of apartment houses these days which don't allow children. Some of them are pretty strict. In my apartment building there's a woman who's so afraid of being evicted, she's in her 14th month.

47. A spinster calls the police. "It's scandalous, that's what it is, absolutely scandalous. Every night the man across the street undresses without pulling down his shade." The police arrive and the sergeant looks out from the spinster's apartment. "I don't see any naked man," he announces. "Of course not," says the spinster. "But just try standing on this bed."

48. A woman had just returned from the hairdresser. Two of her neighbors were discussing the results. "What do you think of it?" asked one. "Well, confidentially, it looks like her parole came through just as the warden pulled the switch."

49. A sexy gal in a bar says, "I'll do anything you want for $200, but say it in three words." A man came forward and said he'd do it. "OK, she says, "but give me the $200 first. Now what is it? "PAINT MY HOUSE."

50. In Osaka, one of Japan's largest cities, my cousin, who's a salesgirl, suddenly came face to face with a middle-aged woman she detests. "My dear! My dear!" said my cousin politely. "What a surprise running into you! I thought you had passed on." "Who told you that?" demanded her enemy. "Nobody," my cousin answered, "but I've heard several people speak well of you lately."

51. I was a den mother escort for a group of Cub Scouts touring a submarine. Ladders provided the only access to the sub, and a sailor was stationed at the foot of each ladder to assist us. Though wearing a billowing skirt, I descended bravely, giving the sailor whatever fringe benefits his duty offered him. Noticing my embarrassment, he grinned and said, "Don't feel too bad, lady. Only married men are stationed at the ladders."

52. A northern woman visiting a friend in the Ozarks was shocked to see her nursing a three-year old child. "That Youngun's too big to be a nursin'", she exclaimed. "It's high time you weaned him." "Don't I know it," was the reply. "But every time I try, he throws rocks at me."

53. Why do women love cats, but hate the same thing in men? Cats are independent, they don't listen, they don't come when you call, they like to stay out all night, they like to be left alone and sleep, but every quality they hate in a man they

70

love in a cat.

54. With 5 shining pennies play this game with friends: "Do you see a per-fume?" "They will say, No. I see a cent." Then place the second one heads up. "Do you see an IQ?" They'll say no. "I see "common cents." Place the third one down. "Do you see any cars?" "They'll say no again. I see a shining Lincoln." Then place the fourth one down. "Do you see any snakes? No, will be the reply again. I see four Copperheads." Last lay the fifth one down. "Do you see the Heather Lochlear in the nude?" After a "no" answer: "Not for five cents, you won't."

Girls

1. Anatomy; Something everybody has, but which always looks better on a girl.

2. Some lovers kiss with their eyes closed. Sometimes, unfortunately they marry the same way.

3. Girl had a little round earring. "Somebody shot you. I still see the BB in your ear."

4. She's so ugly she'd make a freight train take a dirt road.

5. She sent her picture to the lonely hearts' club. They sent it back and said they weren't that lonely.

6. The nicest thing that I can say about her is that all of her tattoos are spelled correctly.

7. The gal at the drug store said that she just don't know how to stop men from following her. Then a customer said, "Just turn around."

8. Good girls go to Heaven–bad girls go everywhere.

9. She's rotten to the core, but very nice to the Calvary.

10. At a queen contest, a man was stationed at the door with a pen to make sure nothing was being falsified. One lady said, "You'd better not stick me with that pen or I'll slap your face." "Don't worry lady. I already have."

11. LONELINESS – I feel so miserable without you, it's almost like having you here. (Stephen Bishop.)

12. I'll get you a blind date. I don't look that bad do I?

13. What's the difference between a man and a parking space? The good ones are taken and the rest of them are handicapped.

14. "Daughter," said the nervous mother, "didn't I tell you never to let men come to your apartment? You know things like that worry me." "I know that," was the reply, "so this time I went to his apartment. Now let his mother worry."

15. "This puzzles me, doctor" complained the nurse. "Every time I lean over to listen to this patient's heart his pulse races. What should I do?" The doctor glanced briefly, then suggested: "Button your collar."

16. A real pretty waitress approached me once and said, "Would you like (to have some) 'Super Sex'?" I got mixed up and took the soup.

PHILOSOPHY

1. The trouble with giving advice is that people want to repay you.
2. I made up my mind, but I made it up both ways. (Yogi Berra.)
3. If you come to a fork in the road, take it.
4. CONVERSATION-It's good to let your mind go blank occasionally, but only if you turn the sound off.
5. I couldn't be two-faced. If I had two faces, I wouldn't wear this one.
6. FAULTS – We don't like people who won't admit their faults, because we would if we had any. (Prochnow.)
7. FRIEND – There are three faithful friends – an old wife, an old dog, and ready money. (Benjamin Franklin.)
8. Early to bed, early to rise, 'til you make enough cash to do otherwise. (Prochnow.)
9. I do unto others what they do unto me, only worse.
10. Do unto others as they do unto you – plus 10 percent.
11. RICH and poor: The poor have more children, but the rich have more relatives. (Anon.)
12. Secret: something you tell one person at a time.
13. The modern home is one in which a switch regulates everything but the children.
14. What's another word for synonym?
15. If a man speaks in the forest, and there is no woman to hear him, is he still wrong?
16. The person who sits around waiting for a break usually winds up broke.
17. Everyone believes in the Golden Rule...Give unto others the advice you can't use yourself.

REUNION

1. Everytime I go to a class reunion, I find my classmates are so fat and bald that they hardly recognize me.
2. Class reunion: Where people get together to see who's falling apart.
3. At a class reunion one classmate had financially excelled all of the rest. Asking him how he had accomplished such success, he said that he uses the Bible. He opened the bible and just plunked his finger down on a word. The first time he put his finger on the word "well." So he purchased an interest in an oil well and became rich. The next time he plunked his finger on the word gold. So he purchased an interest in a South African gold mine and made millions. After the reunion he went to his motel and thought he would see what was in store for him next, so he opened the bible. As he plunked his finger down this time it hit the word Chapter Eleven.

SCHOOL

1. Kid, this is very dangerous. Don't try it at home. I wouldn't even try this at school!

2. A student came late with a note from his mother. "Sorry Andrea is late. The rooster froze up."

3. Wife to husband, reluctantly helping their son with his homework: Help him while you can. Next year he goes into the fourth grade.

4. How many of you were able to make it to school today?

5. The only way I got out of the eighth grade was they passed a law that the father and son can't be in the same grade.

6. It took me two terms to get through the fifth grade. "Yeh, Roosevelt and Truman."

7. "Sex education is O.K. to be taught in school, but they should not be given homework. (Bill Cosby.)

9. John raised his hand for permission to go to the bathroom, but the teacher said, "As soon as we finish this lesson, John." A minute later Andrew, seated right back on John, raised his hand. "I suppose you want permission to leave the room too," the teacher said. "No, I don't" Andrew replied. "I just want to second the motion on John."

10. The little voice on the phone piped up, "Hello, Miss Jones. Johnny Smith isn't feeling well and won't be in school today." "Who is this?" asked the teacher. Back came the voice, "What do you mean who is this? This is my daddy."

11. An Ozark mother asked the third grader why he had come home from school early. He said, "Well it's like this. We had a substitute teacher today and she was really good looking and built just right, and had on a extra-short dress. She dropped an eraser and bent over to get it and James giggled. She turned around and asked him what he was giggling at. He said, "Miss Dorothy, I saw your stockings." She said, "James you get your books and go home and don't come back for two day's." After a while she dropped a piece of chalk, and as she bent over to get it, Earl giggled. She turned around and ask him what he was giggling at. He said, "Miss Dorothy, I saw your garter." "Earl, you get your books and go home and don't you come back for a week." "After a while she dropped a flat ruler, and she bent way, way over to get it. So I just picked up my hat and coat and left, because from what I'd seen, my school days were over."

11. Life was simple in our lifetime. School was simple. When I went to school, we didn't have calculators and computers, all I had was a pencil, and paper and the guy next to me. I'm going to tell you that if that guy setting next to me had of had any sense, no telling what I might have been. (Jim Stafford.)

12. Little Jimmy was strutting into his 1st grade classroom when someone tripped him and he fell flat. "Now, be a big boy and don't cry," soothed his teacher. "Cry, hell," said Jimmy, "I'm gonna sue somebody"

13. "Chickens are the most useful animal," wrote little Tommy in his essay. "You can eat them both before and after they are born."

73

14. Professor: "I take great pleasure in giving you 81 in math." Student: "Why don't you make it a 100 and really enjoy yourself?"

15. "A small boy came up with this defense of his report card: "I was highest of all the kids who failed."

16. The fifth grade teacher took her pupils to the Museum of Natural History. Later, one father asked his son where the teacher had taken him. "Huh," replied the boy disdainfully, "she took us to a dead circus."

17. When I enrolled in a creative-writing course, one of my first poems was returned with the following comment from the teacher: "Put more fire in the poems, or vice versa." (H.A. Maxson.)

18. During our computer class, the teacher chastised one boy for talking to the girl sitting next to him. "I was just asking her a question," the boy said. "If you have a question, ask me," the teacher tersely replied. "Okay," he answered. "Do you want to go out with me Friday night?" (Tracy Maxwell.)

College

1. In the Ozarks, getting a higher education is when the school is sitting on top the hill.

2. A young college boy wrote a heartfelt letter to his parents: Dear Mom and Dad: I'd like to hear from you more often, even if it's only five or ten dollars.

3. Has college been of any value? Sure has. It stopped his mother from bragging on him.

4. A young man was hired by a supermarket and the first job he was asked to do was sweep the floor. But I'm a college graduate. "I'm sorry , I didn't know that. Here, give me the broom, and I'll show you how."

5. As long as there are final exams, there will always be prayers in our schools. (Evan Esar.)

6. It's a shame to waste a college education on a freshman who already knows it all. (Prochnow.)

7. Some lecturers talk in their sleep, but most talk others to sleep. (Evan Esar.)

8. When I went to enter college, my dad asked the dean, "What do you have to offer an Ozark boy like him?" The dean said, "We have English, Trigonometry, Spelling." My dad interrupted with, "Woop, Woop, Woop, give him some of that Trigger Onamy. He's always been the poorest shot in the family."

9. My dad asked the dean if he thought he could make something out of an Ozark boy like me? The dean said, "We made penicillin out of moldy bread, so we can surely make something out of him."

10. I told my first teacher that between my dad and me, we know everything. The professor said, ''OK where's Hayti?'' I said, "That's one of the things my dad knows."

11. I got along good in college until I went to a Home-Ec party one night. I thought I was doing real well with this red-head until I said, "I'll take you home

tonight, honey, if you'll promise not to set me on fire with that pretty red hair." She said, "Don't worry sonny boy, you're too green to burn."

12. I had to write a three-act play in college. Boy meets girl. They hold hands. Boy kisses girl. But the reason I got kicked out of school was that I got all wound up and wrote a five act play.

13. A standard alumni questionnaire with response:

Marital Statu -- Not good.

Wife's Nam --- Plaintiff.

14. An Ozark college student was going to a very hard zoology test that he must pass, or he would have to go to the Army, as well as have to face the fury of his father. As he entered the classroom, he saw the most difficult test that was prepared. Three manikins were covered with only their legs exposed and he had to identify them. He was so angry and disgusted that he stomped up and threw the test on the desk and told the professor that he was the worst teacher in the college and that this was the worst college in the U.S. "Young man, you have just flunked this test. What's your name son?" The student pulled up his pants to show the professor his legs and said, "You guess, professor."

15. ERIC: When it came to education, my father wanted me to have all of the opportunities he never had.

ERNIE: So what did he do?

ERIC: He sent me to a girls' school. (Morecambe and Wise.)

16. A New England youth came here to go to college and said he had been studying English for 19 years, but now that he had moved to the Ozarks, he'd have to start all over again.

17. I got kicked out of college for something that I didn't do. What was that? My homework.

18. I had to laugh when I first heard the greeting on my son's answering machine at College. "Hi, this is Rick. If you are someone from the phone company, I've already sent the money. If this is one of my parents, please send money. If it's my financial institution, you didn't lend me enough money. If you're a friend, you owe me money. If you are a female...I have plenty of money!" (Kristin Clayton.)

SMOKING

1. Smoking is one of the leading causes of statistics.

2. I've gone without smoking so long I feel like a different man. "Yah." (Hitler.)

3. Heavy smokers are in competition with Dr. Kavorkein.

4. Since tobacco was discovered in America, it used to be the only continent that had it. Back then people had a choice of continents. "Smoking or Non-Smoking."

SPEAKER

1. There's a new alarm clock for speakers; it doesn't ring – it applauds.

2. Every speaker hates to be interrupted, except by applause.

3. Did his speech have a happy ending? It sure did. Everybody was mighty happy when it ended.

4. Speaker to his wife: notice how my voice filled the room tonight? "Yes, In fact I noticed many people leaving to make room for it."

5. Shall we have you make your speech now, or should we let the people enjoy themselves a little longer?

6. When people leave during a performance, the speaker can say, "We didn't leave when you got here." That's called a walking ovation.

7. Thanks for being our audience. It's a nasty job, but somebody has to do it.

8. HECKLER: Sir, about your last remark – and I hope it was.

9. Are you going to hear the speech? Yes. It will be boring there. I thought you were the speaker. I am.

10. Emcee gave him a very flattering introduction. After he finished a long boring speech, the emcee rose and said, Mr. Smith, flattery is like perfume. You're just supposed to smell of it, not swallow it.

11. After a long, tiring Thursday night speech, an exhausted listener, asked, "What follows this speaker?" The emcee quietly whispered, "Friday."

12. The job of the public speaker is to talk, the job of the audience is to listen, and the speaker must always finish his job first.

13. There is a car outside with license number 484SVl2287UHA5579BK498. The license plate is blocking the driveway.

14. If you don't think the Lord had a sense of humor, just look at the guy sitting next to you.

15. A speaker's recovery after a crash back stage. "There must be mice in here."

16. Photographer flashes bulb in your face while speaking; "I can still see a little bit out of this other eye, if you would like to take one more picture."

17. The second speaker gigging the first one: John is right when he says he speaks straight from the shoulder. So far as I could tell, none of his ideas originated any higher than that.

18. Response to a dead joke: I just said that to get a laugh; and while we're waiting for it I think I'll try that one on the other side of the house – this side is dead. You might as well laugh now, because this isn't going to get any better. Or a typical emcee response is to peer out from under the spotlight and say to the audience, "I know you're out there – I can hear you breathing."

19. I don't mind if the glass is half full or half empty. I just want to know who's been drinking out of it.

20. "Commencement speakers this year had better not tell the graduates the world is theirs, as has been the habit of these speakers in the past. With the world in the shape it is, they may not want it."

21. "I want to buy all those overripe tomatoes," said a stranger in a smalltown grocery. "Ho, ho," laughed the storekeeper, "I guess you're going to the auditorium to hear that traveling lecturer." "Not so loud," the stranger said, looking around furtively. "I am the lecturer."

22. The after-dinner speaker had talked for fifteen minutes. "After partaking of such a meal," he said, "I feel that if I had eaten any more, I would be unable to the

talk." From the far end of the table came a request: "Give him a sandwich."

INTRODUCTIONS

For An Emcee To Use

1. He is the greatest district manager, a person could have. Of course, he is a little temperamental; about 98% temper and 2% mental.

2. You've heard of the Rambling Wrecks from Georgia Tech? Well, he is our Total Loss From Holy Cross.

3. We refer to him as Moses. Because every time he opens his mouth, the "Bull Rushes."

4. He has won several medals; some gold, some silver, and the next one will be rust.

5. Considered to be one of the best. Of course, considered means it hasn't been decided yet.

6. We never do it the same way twice, and we never have done it right yet.

7. It is my financial pleasure to introduce to you our banker.

8. I want to introduce my little old child bride.

For a Speaker To Use After An Introduction

1. I can't believe all of those nice things you said about me, and I didn't have to die to hear them.

2. You said so many nice things about me that I thought I was at my funeral.

3. There's an old Chinese proverb that goes like this: If you want the baby to be a good singer, you kiss it on the throat. If you want it to be a good scholar, you kiss it on the head. Now I don't know where they kissed Henry, but he sure makes a good chairman.

4. When I was president of Lion's Club and we had ladies night, I thought I was all organized and prepared. As we were ready to sit down to eat, I realized that I hadn't asked anyone to say the blessing. I looked down the table and saw Old Mr. Armstrong. I knew he wouldn't let me down. So I said, "Mr. Armstrong, would you please ask the blessing?" He cupped his hand to his ear and said, "Sonny boy, I can tell you're trying to talk to me, but, I can't tell what the hell you're saying."

5. ACKNOWLEDGING AN EFFUSIVE INTRODUCTION: I only hope I live up to that introduction. After a build-up like that I could be the biggest let-down since Dolly Parton burned her bra.

6. This will be a rather short talk tonight and you can thank three people for it. My partner who took a 45 minute speech and edited it down to 30 minutes, my wife who took the 30 minute speech and edited it down to 15 minutes, and my secretary, who took the 15 minute speech and lost it. .

7. You might call this my Hot Pants Speech. It's shorts but sweet!

8. Material for speakers and toastmasters – Opening – (Come out carrying a magazine.) Good evening, ladies and gentlemen. You'll never guess who made

the center fold of PLAYBOY this month – Maggie Holt!! You think I'm kidding? I'll prove it to you: (PULL OUT A CENTERFOLD THAT IS ACCORDIAN-FOLDED AND AS WIDE AS YOUR ARMS WILL HOLD. IF THERE IS A GOOD-NATURED OVERWEIGHT LADY WHO IS KNOWN TO YOUR AUDIENCE AND DOESN'T MIND BEING KIDDED, USE HER NAME INSTEAD).

9. WHEN SOMEBODY GOOFS YOUR INTRODUCTION: it could be worse. Last week a master of ceremonies introduced me by saying, "And now we bring you the latest dope from Howell county."

10. After hearing himself introduced in extravagantly flowery and glowing terms, the guest speaker said: "That introduction reminds me of the man who, on Judgment Day, stuck his head out of the grave, read his epitaph in wonderment, and exclaimed: "Either somebody is a terrible liar...or I'm in the wrong hole!"

SPORTS

Camping

1. A camper is the same guy who pays a stiff fee for the same sort of uncomfortable accommodations he griped about in the army.

2. His idea of roughing it is to turn his electric blanket down to medium. (Anon.)

3. I rode a horse and it's not my neck that's red. (Yakoff.)

Fishing

1. The fishing is real good here. They are hitting so fast that you have to get behind a tree to bait your hook.

2. We should mark this good fishing place. Let's just put an X on the boat. That's silly. What if we would get another boat?

3. A tourist in the Ozarks said that this is the darndest country that he ever saw. There is a boy in the timber way up on top of that hill a fishing. What's wrong with him? The boy's dad said, "Don't know. I'll get the boat and go get him."

4. Cooking carp. Roll and bake them in fresh cow manure. Bake them until they are real crisp. Then throw away the carp and eat the cow manure.

5. "This river is the foggiest place in the world." "I've been to a place foggier than this." "Where was that?" "I don't know. It was too foggy to tell."

6. A young boy of five was fishing in a bucket in his front yard when a passerby stopped and asked, with a twinkle in his eye: "How many have you caught, young fellow?" "You're the third," the boy replied.

7. Angler (to friend) Yes, the fish was too small to bother with, so I got two men to throw it back into the water.

8. A fortunate fisherman lugging a tremendous fish up the dock met another fisherman with a half dozen small ones on a string. "Howdy," said the fortunate

one, dropping his big fish and waiting for the bug-eyed one to comment. But he was denied his moment of glory. The other fisherman, green-eyed with jealousy, held himself together, stared calmly and remarked cooly, "Just caught the one, eh?"

9. The fishing party was hopelessly lost in deep woods, with supplies running low. "I thought you claimed to be the best guide in Wisconsin," said one man, "I am," shrugged the guide, "but now I think we're somewhere in Manitoba."

10. When looking at the big fish that was hanging on his client's office wall he said, "Whoever caught that one is a liar."

11. The one armed fisherman was showing the boys how big a fish he had caught by holding out one arm and one hand.

12. My sister ran a for-sale ad in our local newspaper asking $200 for her small boat, motor and trailer. She received several calls, but no one came by. Then she changed the ad to read, "Small boat and motor for sale – $200. Will throw in boat trailer for free." The equipment was sold the same day. (Shirley Martin.)

Games

1. A college professor walked up to a football player who was obviously experiencing difficulty with a math examination. "Having trouble, son?" asked the professor. "Yeah," answered the athlete. "I sure am!" "Well," said the professor, trying to be helpful," how far are you from the right answers?" The ball player gave a quick look around the room at some of his classmates. "About four seats," he said.

2. The coach put in the cross eyed discus thrower; not to set any records, but just to keep the crowd alert.

3. Did you hear about the All-American Tom Cat? He made 47 yards in one night.

4. Make sure both of you throw the ball simultaneously and at the same time.

5. I left three Cowboy tickets in a locked car. Someone broke in and left three more.

6. Baseball is 90% mental. The other half is physical. (Yogi Berra.)

7. We made too many wrong mistakes.

8. Michael Jordan scored 69 points at the last game, then I substituted for him and made one point. The media asked me later, "what is the most important time of your life?" When Michael Jordon and I scored 70 points in one game."

9. A baseball manager died and went to Heaven and was placed in charge of the great team. But there was no other team to play. The devil called and wanted to play his team. Sure, but we'll beat the pants off of you, because we have the best team of all times. Maybe so, the devil said, but remember, I've got all of the umpires.

10. During my first deer hunt, two hours passed and nothing happened. The deer showed and I screamed, and the deer ran away. I told my wife, I'm sorry I didn't mean to do that. I was real quiet when the skunk squirted me, and when the snake crossed my legs,

I kept quiet. But when that squirrel ran up my leg and started storing for the winter. – (Yakoff.)

11. Texans carry rifles in their pickup racks. Ozarkers carry a Cruise Missile.

12. An excited fan had been cheering his team to victory all through the game. He suddenly turned to his companion and whispered, "I've lost my voice." His companion replied, "Don't worry. You'll find it in my left ear."

13. Any baseball team could use a man who plays every position superbly, who never strikes out, and never makes an error but there's no way for the manager to make him lay down his hot dog and come out of the grandstand.

Golf

1. Golf, golf, golf. I'd drop dead if you spent one Sunday at home. You can't bribe me now.

2. As the sweet young thing took a golf lesson, "Now which club do I use for a hole in one." (Prochnow.)

3. My boss insisted that I go play golf. My score was 88. We didn't play the second hole.

Hunting

1. An angry wife said, Jim, one of those pheasants you were hunting last fall called up today and left her phone number."

2. Eddie was trying to sell a gun and he was making a sales pitch. I kicked up 100 birds and the gun is so good that I killed 99 at one shot. "If you are going to tell a story that big, you just as well kill the whole 100." His wife said, "Eddie isn't going to lie for just one bird."

3. A FRIEND: Two hunters saw a Grizzly Bear coming for them and the first hunter sit right down and took his hunting boots off and put on his running shoes. The second hunter said, "Why are you doing that? You can't outrun that bear." The first hunter said, "I won't have to. All I have to do is outrun is you."

4. An Ozarker wrote the Wildlife Department and ask them to please take down those "Deer Crossing" signs. He said too many deer are being killed along there.

5. An Ozarker said that he ate a Blue Heron. "You're not supposed to eat them. They're almost extinct." "What did it taste like?" "Tasted sort of like a Bald Eagle to me.

6. In the Ozarks, they evaluate the economy by the number of deer heads and large bass people have hanging on their walls.

7. If you see rifles mounted in the rear window on an old rusty pickup truck that's never been washed, you're probably getting close to the Ozarks.

8. At an Ozark fox hunt, they were using all-male hounds, except one female, which was in heat. One of the hunters was asked, "Did you see the hounds go by?" "Yap." "See where they went?" "Nope. But it was the first time I ever seen a fox running fifth."

9. The novice trying out for the rifle team did very poorly in his first test. Turn

80

ing in his score card, he blurted out, "I think I'll go home and shoot myself." The team captain studied the score card carefully, then replied, "Better take two bullets."

10. "Is it true," the teenager asked of the explorer just returned from Africa, "that lions won't hurt you if you carry a torch?" "That depends," replied the explorer, "on how fast you carry it."

Skiing

1. I went sky diving. I did OK, but should have worn brown pants. (Yakoff)
2. Ski instructor to pupil in training: "You just don't seem to get the hang of it, Mr. Smedley. Now you've broken a ski instead of a leg."

Swimming

1. Sign: Swimming pool is open 24 hours. Please do not enter at any other time.
2. A girl was swimming nude in the park. The park attendant came by and said, "there's no swimming allowed here." the girl said, "Why didn't you tell me that before I undressed?" He sheepishly replied, "Oh, there's no law against undressing."

TEXAS

1. You can always tell a Texan, but you can't tell him much.
2. Ross Perot has a famous brother in Springfield, MO. – "'Bass Pro."
3. Ross Perot Corn–Doesn't grow very much corn, but has big ears.
4. My nephew Bill writes from Texas that a man with a mink farm there is trying to cross his minks with kangaroos, so he can raise fur coats with pockets.
5. An operator from Texas was telling an operator from Alberta about the wonderful fishing in Texas. "Why just last week," said the Texas skinner, "I caught a trout that measured nine inches." "That's a small fish in Alberta," said the Canadian. "Yeah, but where I come from we measure them between the eyes," reported the tall Texan.
6. A Boston salesman visited Texas and heard one particular Texan boasting about heroes of the Alamo who, almost alone, held off whole armies. "I'll bet you never had anybody so brave around Boston," challenged the Texan. "Did you ever hear of Paul Revere?" asked the Bostonian. "Paul Revere?" said the Texan. "Isn't that the young man who ran for help?"
7. A Texan who was fond of playing practical jokes sent a friend a telegram, charges collect, which read: "I am perfectly well." About a week later, the joker received a heavy package on which he was required to pay very considerable charges. Opening it, he found a big block of concrete on which was pasted the message: "This is the weight your telegram lifted from my mind."

TRAMPS

1. "Beg your pardon ma-am, do you have some pie or cake you could spare an unfortunate wanderer?" "No, I'm afraid not. Wouldn't some bread and butter do?" "As a general rule it would ma-am, but you see, this is my birthday."

WEATHER

1. It's so cold up here that if you cut yourself, you'll have to wait until spring to see if you are going to bleed.

2. At seeing a man walking waist deep in snow.. Aren't you in bad shape? If you think I'm in bad shape, you should see my horse.

3. It's so windy here that there are whitecaps on the horse trough.

4. Teacher (to a weatherman's son) "What are two and two?" Weatherman's son: "Four.. probably.

5. My wife has already started spring housecleaning. This morning she started with my wallet.

6. During a recent hot spell in the Ozarks, a hillbilly collapsed on the street. Immediately a crowd gathered and began offering suggestions,"Give the poor man a drink of whiskey" a little old lady said. "Give him some air," a man called out. "Give him some whiskey," she cried again. Several other suggestions were made and the victim suddenly sat up and hollered, "Will all of you shut up and listen to the little old lady?"

7. A visitor to a Western hotel asked the clerk about the weather. The clerk had no information, but an Indian standing near by came up with the answer, "Going rain-much." And so it did. Awed by the Indian's accuracy, the visitor sought him out the next day for another prediction, and learned it was to be clear and cool. Again the forecast was correct. The third morning the query was repeated, but this time the Indian smiled and said, "Dunno – radio broke."

8. "They tell me it gets pretty cold up here in the winter." "Yeah it does. You know that statue of Lincoln, standing up in the park, with his hand on a little boy's head? Well, last winter it got so cold he stuck his hand in his pocket to warm them."

P.S.

1. Be nice to your kids. Remember, they pick out your nursing home.

2. The only thing I do behind my wife's back is zip her up.

3. Politicians are just like diapers. Need to be changed often & for the same reason.

4. Can you really afford to give anybody a piece of your mind?

5. If they can put one man on the moon, why not all of them?

6. Shin: A very sensitive device for finding furniture in the dark.

7. Don't eat onions and beans. You'll get tear gas.

8. Mom, are you having a bad day? Call 1-800-Grandma.

9. If at first you don't succeed … sky diving is probably not for you.

10. Bought a new chain saw. Run an ad in paper, "For sale - only used one time - Call and ask for "Lefty."

11. You have a cough? Go home tonight, eat a whole box of Ex-Lax. Tomorrow you'll be afraid to cough. Pearl Williams

12. They think they can make fuel from horse manure … Now I don't know if your car will be able to get thirty miles to the gallon, but it's sure gonna put a stop to siphoning. Bille Holliday

13. You have to stay in shape. My grandmother, she started walking give miles a day when she was 60. She's 97 today and we don't know where the hell she is. Ellen Degeneris

14. To their four year old son as they started out for the evening, "OK I won't call a baby-sitter if you promise to spend the whole evening working on Daddy's web site."

15. Talk is cheap because the supply always exceeds the demand.

16. Now doctor, isn't it true that when a person dies in his sleep, he doesn't know about it until the next morning?

17. Watching the TV means fighting, violence and foul language … and that's just deciding who gets to hold the remote control.

18. "I told my doctor that ever time I look in the mirror I get sick," says Rodney Dangerfield. "He told me, 'At least your eyesight is good.'"

19. A wealthy man came home from a gambling trip and told his wife that he had lost their entire fortune and that they would have to drastically alter their life-style. " If you will just learn to cook," he said, "we can fire the chef."

"Fine." She said. "And if you learn how to make love, we can fire the gardener."

20. Two men were sitting in a doctor's office. "What are you in here for?" asked on. "Circumcision," came the reply.

"I had one of those done the day after I was born," the first man commented. "Afterward I couldn't walk for a year."

21. Mother to her young son. "Well, I don't believe for one minute that the school is cutting back and you got laid off."

22. The second day of a diet is always easier than the first. By the second day you're off it. Jackie Gleason

23. Never raise your hands to your kids. It leaves your groin unprotected. Red Buttons

24. I have a daughter who goes to SMU. She could've gone to UCLA here in California, but it's one more letter she'd have to remember. Shecky Green

25. A conference is a gathering of important people who singly can do anything, but together can decide that nothing can be done. Fred Allen

26. Everything is drive-through. In California they even have a burial service called Jump-In-The-Box. Wil Shriner

27. When I was little, my folks used to take me shopping with them. That way they could park in the handi-capped section. Rodney Dangerfield

28. Is that child spoiled? No, he always smells that way.

29. He likes girls so much that he is going to be president some day.

30. He is learning to an astronaut in school - he's taking up space.

31. I'm desperately trying to figure out why kamikaze pilots wore helmets. Dave Edison.

32. Diplomacy is the art of saying "Nice doggie" until you can find a rock. Will Rogers.

33. Don't drive as if you own the road; drive as if you own the car.

34. If it weren't for electricity we'd all be watching television by candlelight. George Gobel.

35. Pluber to lady client; "Ma'am, this is your bill, plus $50 for your husband helping me."

36. A word to the wife is sufficient to start a quarrel.

37. A domestic quarrel often ends with the husband having his hands full - of flowers.

38. In the days of pioneering the west, Jake and Izzy were travelling through Colorado by stage coach. Suddenly the stage stopped, and Jake realized that robbers were about to stage a hold-up. Quickly, Jake took some money from his wallet and handed it to his companion, Izzy, he explained, Here is the fifty dollars I owe you.

39. Definition of a pessimist: An optimist who is in possession of all the facts.

40. A scientifically-minded young man sat up all night trying to figure out where the sun went when it went down. Finally it dawned on him.

41. The trouble with being an expert is that you can't turn to anybody else for advice.

42. All you really have to do if you want the world to beat a path to your door is lie down to take a nap.

43. "What's the difference between a tenured professor and a terrorist?" "The terrorist, you can negotiate with."

44. Did you hear about the teacher who retired and lost all her principals?

45. I was a vegetarian for a while, but I quit because there are side effects. I found myself sitting in my living room, starting to lean toward the sunlight. Rita Rudner

46. A young man said to his father, "I want to marry a wife who is real smart." His father said, "Ok." "I want to marry a wife who is beautiful." "Ok." "I want to marry a woman that will make me happy." The father said, " Make up your mind."

47. Instead of tooting your own horn, get someone else to do it. The sound will travel twice as far.

48. Hillary is changing her name to Share.

49. Hillary has hired her own intern … Lorena Bobbitz!!!

50. CEO to branch manager, "Henry, I need you to write a report on how much this company can save by eliminating your job."

51. Is it because light travels faster than sound that some people appear bright until they speak?

52. Don't knock the weather; do you realize how many people couldn't start a conversation if it didn't change once in a while?

53. Last year I planted okra on the north side of the house. The north wind froze my okra. This year I planted it on the south side of the house, where the north wind

couldn't get to it. That gives me "Okra Wind Free." Wednesdays at 4:00 p.m.

54. Negotiating for a mink coat: If I buy the coat and I get caught in the rain, will it get ruined? Look, lady, did you ever see a mink carrying an umbrella?

55. Abe said to his friend Willie, Willie, lend me twenty dollars. Willie took out his wallet and handed Abe a ten dollar bill. Willie, said Abe, I asked you for twenty. Yes, I know, said Willie. This way you lose ten and I lose ten.

56. All the girls from the office poured into a crowded cafeteria for the coffee break. One of the girls lit a cigarette and blew ring after ring of smoke. An elderly lady, sitting next to her, was supremely annoyed. Miss, she said, that smoking is a horrible habit. I would rather commit adultery than smoke.

So would I, answered the girl, but, you know, there just isn't time during a coffee break.

57. Some young man is trying to get into my room through my window, screamed spinster into the telephone.

Sorry, lady, came back the answer, you've got the fire department. What you want is the police department.

Oh, no, she pleaded, I want the fire department. What he needs is a longer ladder.

58. A few years ago with the Fourth of July approaching, it was my job as safety officer of my Marine Corps unit to develop a slogan and to put up posters discouraging drinking over the holiday weekend. We had no accidents that year, and I attribute it partly to our slogan: "He who comes forth with a fifth on the Fourth may no come forth on the fifth." Robert Abney

59. During our family vacation, we were outside admiring the shoreline. Suddenly we saw a group of parachutes in brightly colored gear floating in the sky. A young single woman, a guest of the family, was wide-eyed. "This must be heaven," she said. "It's raining men!!"

60. My doctor told me that I would live two years longer if I would quit eating donuts. Which is best, my way or his? My way, I can eat donuts until I die. His way, I've got two more years without doughnuts!!

61. Speaker to crowd - If laughter makes you live longer, some of you aren't going to make it through the night.

62. Nice lady was touring some people - in the horse stalls, a horse passed gas - lady apologized, was so sorry. Little by in tour said, "Lady, if you hadn't said anything, I'd of thought it was the horse.

63. I've eaten so much fiber now, I'm passing liquid furniture

64. A sign in a nursery, We Guarantee Our Plants To Grow - Or Die Trying.

65. Dr. - You only have 6 months to live. Take a mud bath. Will it cure me? No, but it will get you used to the dirt. He was an HMO Dr.

66. A lady was walking down the street.
Suddenly a voice said stop.
She stopped and a brick fell in her path.
On down the street, a voice said stop.
She stopped and a beer truck run right in her path.
She said, "Who are you?" "I am your guardian angel. An I guess there are some questions you want to ask me."

"Yes. Where were you on my wedding day?"

67. A woman answered her front door and found two boys holding a list.

"Lady," one of them explained, "we are on a treasure hunt, and we need three grains of wheat, a pork-chop bone and piece of used carbon paper to earn a dollar."

"Wow," the woman replied. "Who sent you on such a challenging hunt?"

"Our babysitter's boyfriend."

68. The little boy came home from Sunday School and told his mom that his Sunday School teacher was Christ's mother. "Why is that, Johnny?" "Because she must have had 30 pictures of Him, and she showed them all the time.

69. In a domestic quarrel there's only one way to convince your wife, and that is to agree with her.

70. Compromise is the art of dividing a pie so that each person believes he got the biggest slice.

71. Remember that as a teenager, you are in the last stage of your life where you will be happy to hear the phone is for you. Fran Lebowitz

72. At the coffee shop, Henry asked Uncle John, "My mule is sick, what should I do. I sure hate to loose him. He is my work mule, riding mule and hunting mule. It is impossible to replace a mule like that." Uncle John replied, "I had a mule that got sick like that and I gave him a quart of Turpentine." So Henry directly went home and gave his mule a quart of Turpentine, but his mule promptly died. The next morning at the coffee shop he immediately said to Uncle John, "I gave my mule a quart of Turpentine, like you said, but he died!" Uncle John replied, "That doesn't surprise me. My mule died too."

73. The plaintiff's lawyer asked the little old lady witness, "Do you know me? She said, "Yes, and I'm very disappointed in you. You divorced your wife and you won't pay the alimony, and you don't go to church." The lawyer asked her if she knew the defense's attorney. She said, "Yes, and I'm very disappointed in him. He gets drunk, gambles, and will not support his family, and he doesn't go to church." At that the judge called the two lawyers over to the bench, and said to them, "Don't either one of you ask her if she knows me, or I'll have to dismiss you."

74. A famous scientist was on his way to yet another lecture when his chauffeur offered an idea. "Hey, boss, I've heard your speech so many times, I bet I could deliver it for you and give you a night off."

"Sounds great," the scientist said.

When they got to the auditorium, the scientist put on the chauffeur's hat and settled into the back row. The chauffeur walked to the lectern and delivered the speech. Afterward he asked if there were any questions.

"Yes," said one professor. The he launched into a highly technical question.

The chauffeur was panic-stricken for a moment but quickly recovered.

"That's an easy one," he replied. "So easy, I'm going to let my chauffeur answer it."

75. When a man in Macon, Ga. came upon a wild dog attacking a young boy, he quickly grabber the animal and throttled it with his two hands. A reporter saw the incident, congratulated the man and told him what the headline the following day would read, "Local Man Saves Child by Killing Vicious Animal."

The hero, however, told the journalist he wasn't from Macon.

"Well, then," they reporter said, "the headline will probably say, 'Georgia Man Saves Child by Killing Dog'."

"Actually," the man said, "I'm from Connecticut."

"In that case," the reporter said in a huff, "the headline will read, 'Yankee Kills Family Pet'."

76. When my daughter took part in her first high school debate, I was there for moral support. The debate's topic was "Cooperation or Competition," and my daughter was to argue for cooperation. She tool a deep breath and began: "If my mom and dad had been competing instead of cooperating, I wouldn't be standing here tonight."

77. One March day my wife said that the house needed painting. "It's still winter," I replied.

"Forget it."

In April, she told me she had bought some exterior latex. I said that it was still too cool to paint.

In May, I heard her outside one day yelling for help, and we set up the ladder so she could start painting. Then I went inside to get a beer. As I sat in a lawn chair not far from where m wife was working, a neighbor passed by. "Aren't you ashamed?" she asked. "How can you sit there drinking beer while your wife is up on a ladder painting the house?"

Glancing up at my wife, I responded, "She doesn't like beer."

78. Two brothers, Jim and Joe, lived in Oklahoma, and Joe moved to Detroit and became very wealth. There father became very ill and Jim alone took great care of him until he died. Joe told Jim to send him all of the funeral bills, because that's the lease he could do. Jim sent Joe the bill, and it was paid. Then Jim sent Joe a bill for $75.80, and Joe told his secretary to just pay it, that it was something that Jim probably just overlooked. The next month Joe got another bill for $78.50 and Joe just paid it also. The next month, Joe got another bill for the same amount. He finally called Jim and asked him about it. Jim said that their dad always wanted to be buried in a tuxedo, but he couldn't afford it, so he just rented him one. Dr. Don Gose

DUMB BLONDE JOKES

79. She thought a quarter back was a refund.

80. She tripped over a cordless phone.

81. She spent 20 minutes looking at the orange juice box, because it said concentrate.

82. She put lipstick on the forehead, because she wanted to make up her mind.

83. She got stabbed in a shootout.

84. She told me to meet her at the corner of "Walk" and "Don't Walk."

85. She took a ruler to bed to see how long she slept.

86. If she spoke her mind, she'd probably be speechless.

87. She studied for a blood test and failed.

88. When she heard that 90% of all crimes occur around the home, she moved.

89. She thinks Taco Bell is where you pay you phone bill.

90. When she took you to the airport and saw a sign that said "Airport Left," she

turned around and went home.

91. Q: Doctor, before you performed the autopsy, did you check for a pulse?
A: No.
Q: Did you check for blood pressure?
A: No.
Q: Did you check for breathing?
A: No.
Q: So, then it is possible that the patient was alive when you began the autopsy?
A: No.
Q: How can you be so sure, Doctor?
A: Because hi brain was sitting on my desk in a jar.
Q: But could the patient have still been alive nevertheless?
A: It is possible that he could have been alive and practicing law some where. (Kenna Cameron)

92. Mr. and Mrs. Mandelbaum decided the only solution to their marital problems was in divorce. So they went to see the rabbi.

The rabbi was concerned about the three children and was reluctant to see the family broken up. He thought that if he could stall the couple maybe they would work it out together.

Well, said the rabbi, there's no way of dividing three children. What you'll have to do is live together one more year. You'll have a fourth child, and then, it will be easy to arrange a proper divorce. You'll take two children, and he'll take two.

Nothing doing, said Mrs. Mandelbaum. Rabbi, if I depended on him, I wouldn't have had these three!

93. A very successful businessman had a meeting with his new son-in-law. "I love my daughter," he said, "and now I welcome you into the family. To show you how much we care for you, I'm making you a 50-50 partner in my business. All you have to do is go to the factory everyday and learn the operations."

The son-in-law interrupted him. "I hate factories. I can't stand all the noise." "I hat office work," countered the young man. "I can't stand being stuck behind a desk all day."

"Wait a minute," the exasperated father-in-law said. "I just made you half owner of a money making organization, but you say you don't like factories and won't work in the office. What am I going to do with you?"

"Easy," said the smug son-in-law. "Buy me out."

94. Each year on Father's Day our pastor tries to locate the oldest father in the group. He first asks all the father to stand, then asks the men in their 20s to sit, then the men in their 30s and so on. When he gets to the 70s, the pastor goes year by year. Last year he finally got into the 90s, and my father and one other man were standing. The pastor called out, "Ninety-four," and when my father sat down, obviously disappointed, he whispered to my daughter, "Darn, that guy beats me every year!"

 95. Stepping out of the shower one morning, a beautiful young women wrapped herself in a towel and tells her husband it's his turn to use the shower. Just then, the doorbell rings, so she goes to the door.

It's their neighbor, Bill, whose jaw drops at the sight of the lovely bride wrapped only in a towel. He pulls out two hundred-dollar bills and says they're hers if she'll drop the towel down to the waist. We could really use $200, she thinks, and drops the towel a few inches. Bill gasps at the sight and pulls out two more hundreds and offers them to her, too, if she'll drop the towel all together.

Well. I've already compromised my self, she thinks, so what the heck. She lets the towel fall to the floor, and Bill gets a good look. She quickly takes the money. Bill thanks her and leaves. She goes back upstairs as her husband is getting out of the shower. "Who was at the door, honey?" he asks.

When she tells him it was Bill, he asks, "did he say anything about the $400 he owes me?" Richard Wright

96. The company I work for recently purchased a building that had once been a hospital. Management asked for volunteers to help with some light, renovation. I joined up, and my first task was to take signs down in the parking lot. One read, "Reserved for Physician." I said to a co-worker that I should keep the sign and post it on my sister's garage door. My friends asked, "Is your sister a doctor?" "No," I replied. "She's single." John Allen, Waxahachie, Texas.

97. THINKING; The campers were exhausted after their long hike home, except for one particular guy who showed no signs of being tired.

"How come you're not pooped out like your camping buddies are? his father asked.

"Well, I remember when you always told me to smarten up. So when we planned the trip we agreed whatever each of us carried into the woods we carry back out."

"I guess that's fair enough," his father said, "but where does the smart part come in?"

"Well, they all thought I was crazy when I volunteered to carry in all the food." Hal Borden

98. A drill sergeant ordered two young female recruits to paint a room in the barracks, stressing that they not get any paint on their uniforms. Doubtful they could avoid ruining their clothes, the women locked the door, stripped naked and painted in the nude. After about an hour they heard a knock at the door. "Who is it?" asked one of the women. "Blind man," came the reply.

Seeing no harm in letting blind men in, they opened the door.

"Woe, what knockouts!" the man said with surprise. "Now, where do you want these blinds?"

99. ACTUAL QUESTIONS FROM COURT HOUSE TRIALS
Q: So the date of conception (of the baby) was August 8?
A: Yes.
Q: And what were you doing at that time?

Q: You say the stairs went down to the basement?
A: Yes.
Q: And these stairs, did they go up also?

Q: Mr. Slatery, you went on a rather elaborate honeymoon, didn't you?

A: I went to Europe, Sir.
Q: And you took your wife?

Q: How was your first marriage terminated
A: By death.
Q: And by who's death was it terminated.

Q: Can you describe the individual?
A: He was about medium height and had a beard.
Q: Was he male, or female
Q: So you recall the time that you examined the body?
A: The autopsy started around 8:30 p.m.
Q: And Mr. Dennin was dead at the time?
A: No, he was sitting on the table wondering why I was doing an autopsy. Kenna Cameron

INVESTMENT 2000

I don't know if you would be interested in this, but I thought I would mention it to you because it could be a real "sleeper" in making a lot of money with very little investment.

A group of us are considering investing in a large cat ranch near Karmossillo, Mexico. It is our purpose to start rather small, with about one million cats. Each cat averages about twelve kittens a year; skins can be sold for about 20 cents for the white ones and up to 40 cents for the black. This will give us 12 million cat skins per year to sell at an average price of around 32 cents making our revenue about $3 million a year. This really averages out to $10,000 a day – excluding Sundays and holidays.

A good Mexican cat man can skin about 50 cats per day at a wage of $3.15 a day. It will only take 663 men to operate the ranch so the net profit will be over $8,200 per day.

Now the cats would be fed on rats exclusively. Rats multiply four times as fast as cats. We would start a rat ranch right adjacent to our cat farm. If we start with a million rats, we would have four rats per cat per day. The rats will be fed on the carcasses of the cats we skin. This will give each rat one quarter of cat. You can see by this that the business is a clean operation, self-supporting and really automatic throughout. The cats will eat the rats and the rats will eat the cats and we will get the skins.

Let me know if you are interested; as you can imagine, we are rather particular who we want to get into this, and want the fewest investors possible.

Eventually, it is our hope to cross the cats with snakes, for they will skin themselves twice a year. This would save the labor costs of skinning as well as give us two skins for one cat.

GOOD SAMARITAN

A black man from one of the southern states desired to enter the Ministry. He went to a Minister to be examined and the following conversation took place, "Can you read,Sam?" "Nossah, ah can't read, sah". – "Can you write?" – "Well no sah, ah can't write, but, de ole'ooman is a good writer". – "Well, do you know your Bible, Sam? – " O,yassah, ah's smart in the Bible ,sah". – "Tell me,what part of the Bible do you prefer!"-_" Well, I prefers the New Testement, sah". " And what do you like in the New Testement, Sam?" – " De Book of Mark, sah." "And what do you like especially about Mark?" – "I like the parables de bes' sah". – "And which of the parables is your choice?. "Well sah, de parable of de good Samaritan is mah Special Favorite sah ah likes dat one de best".

"Well Sam, will you tell me a story of the goad Samaritan? – " Yessah, I sho will sah". – – "Once upon a time a man was a goin' from Jerusalem to Jericho an' he fell among the thorns. De thorns grew up an' chocked him, an' he went on an' didn't have any money. An' he went to de Queen of Sheba, an' she gave him, a thousand talents of money, an' a hundred of raiment. An den he got in a chariot an' drove furiously. An when he was drivin' under a big Juniper tree, his har done got caught in de limb of de tree, and he hung dar, an' hung dar many days, an' de ravens brought him food to eat an' water to drink, an' afterwards he was an hungared, an' he ate five thousan' loaves of bread and two small fishes. An' one night while he was ahangen'dar, asleep his wife Delilah came alng an' cut off his har an' he dropped an'fell on stony ground, but he got up an'went on, an'went on, an'it rained forty days and forty nights an' he hid hisself in a cave, an' lived on locust an' wild honey. Den he went on till he met a servant who said, "Come take supper at mah house," an' he begin to make excuses an' said," No I wont, I married a wife an' I can't go". An' de servant went out in the highway an' hedges an' compel him to come in. An' after super he went on an' come to Jericho. An' when he got dar he looked an' saw Queen Jesebelle sittin' a way up in a winder, an' she laff at him, an' he said, "Thro her down", an' they throw'd her down, an' he said, thro her down some more, an' so they thro her down sebenty times seban. And of the fragments they picked up twelve baskets full. An' at Razzerection day, who's wife am she????????? .

LAST WILL AND TESTAMENT

Last will and testament of Herman Oberweiss offered for probate at the June term 1934 of the County Court.

I am writing of my last will mineself that des lawyer wand he should have to much money he ask to many answers about the family.

First think I want done I don't want my brother Oscar got a gosh dam thing.

I got he is a mumser he done me out of four dollars fourteen years since.

want it that Hilda my sister she gets the North Sixtie akers at where I am hom-ing it now. I bet she don't get that loafer husband of hers to brake twenty akers next plowing. She want have it if she lets Oscar live on it I want I should have it back if she does.

Tell mama that six hundred dollars she has been looking for ten years is berried from the backhouse behind about ten feet down. She better let little Fredrick do the digging and count it when he comes up.

Pastor Licknitz can have three hundret dollars, if he kisses the book he wont preach no dumhed talks about politiks. He should a roof put on the meeting house with the elders should the bills look at.

Mama should the rest get, but I want it so that Adolph tell her what not she sould do so no more slik irishers sell her vacken cleaner, they noise like hell and a broom don't cost so much.

want it that mine brother Adolph be my executor and I want that the Judge should please make Adolph plenty bond put and watch him like hell. Adolph is a good bizness man but only a dumkolph would trust him with a blasted pfennig.

want dam sure that Schleimial Oscar don't nothing get, tell Adolph he can have a hundret dollars if he prove to Judge Oscar don't get nothing. That dam sure fix Oscar.

Herman Oberweiss

NOT RAISING HOGS

Following is a copy of a letter from Octave Broussard of Louisiana to Ezra Taft Benson, Secretary of Agriculture:

Dear Mr. Secretary:

My friend Bordeau over in Terrebonne Parish received A $1,000 check from the government this year for not raising hogs. So, I want to go into the "not raising hogs" business next year.

What I want to know is, in your opinion, what is the best kind of farm not to raise hogs on, and what is the best breed of hogs not to raise. I want to be sure that I approach this endeavor in keeping with all government policies. I would prefer not to raise razorbacks, but if that is not a good breed to not raise, then I will just as gladly not raise Tamworth or Berkshires,

As I see it, the hardest part of this program will be in keeping an accurate inventory of how many hogs I haven't raised.

My friend Bordeau is very joyful about the future of this business. He has been raising hogs for twenty years or so, and the best he ever made on them was $422 in 1968, until this year when he got your check for $1,000 for not raising hogs.

If I can get $1,000 for not raising 50 hogs, will I get $2,000 for not raising 100 hogs? I plan to operate on a small scale at first, holding myself down to about 4,000 hogs not raised, which will mean about $80,000 the first year. Then I can afford an airplane.

Now another thing, these hogs I will not raise, will not eat 100,000 bushels of corn. I understand that you also pay farmers for not raising corn. Will I qualify for payments for not raising corn not to feed the 4,000 hogs I am not going to raise?

Also, I'm considering the "Not Milking Cows" business, so send me any information you have on that too.

I want to get started as soon as possible as this seems to be a good time of the year not to raise hogs. At least it seems to me this is better than working in a broker's office and I hope you understand my feelings on the subject. I have a lot to learn about not raising things, but I'm young and willing to do it. If things go well, I may even get married and not raise any children. I haven't checked what the government pays for not raising them, but surely it must be more than they pay for not raising hogs.

In view of these circumstances, you understand that I will be totally unemployed and plan to file for unemployment and food stamps. Can I raise 10 or 12 hogs on the side while I am in the not-raising-hog-business – just enough to get me a few sides of bacon to eat?

Be assured you will have my vote in the coming election.

Patriotically Yours,
Octave Broussard

P. S. Would you please notify me when you plan to distribute more free cheese?

A LOOK BACK

For Those Born Before 1954...The Survivors

As we move into another year, and become a year older, a depressing thought until one considers the alternative, we wanted to share these thought provoking facts.

We were born before television, before penicillin, before polio shots, frozen foods, Zerox, plastic, contact lenses, Frisbees and the Pill. We were before radar, credit cards, split atoms, laser beams and ball-point pens. Before pantyhose, dishwashers, clothes dryers, electric blankets, air conditioners, drip dry clothes...and before man walked on the moon.

We got married first and then lived together. How quaint can you be? In our time, closets were for clothes, not for "coming out of." Bunnies were small rabbits, and rabbits were not Volkswagons. Designer Jeans, were scheming girls named Jean, and having a meaningful relationship meant getting along with our cousins.

We thought fast food was what you ate during lent, and outer space was the back of the Riviera Theatre. We were before house husbands, gay rights, computer dating, dual careers and computer marriages. We never heard of FM radio, tape decks, electronic typewriters, artificial hearts, word processors, yogurt and guys wearing earrings. For us, time-sharing meant togetherness..not computers or condominiums. A chip meant a piece of wood. Hardware meant hardware, and software wasn't even a word.

Back then, "Made in Japan" meant junk, "making out" referred to how you did on your exam. Pizzas, McDonald's and instant coffee were unheard of. We hit the scene where there were 5 and 10 cent stores, where you bought things for five and ten cents. Sanders or Wilsons sold ice cream cones for a nickel or a dime. For a nickel you could ride a street car, make a phone call, buy a Pepsi, or enough stamps to mail one letter and two postcards. You could buy a Chevy Coupe for $600...but who could afford one? A pity too, because gas was 11 cents a gallon.

In our day, grass was mowed. Coke was a cold drink and Pot was something you cooked in. Rock music was a grandmas lullaby and AIDS were helpers in the principal's office. We were certainly not before the difference between the sexes was discovered, but we were surely before the sex change. We made do with what we had. And we were the last generation that was so dumb as to think you needed a husband to have a baby. No wonder we are so confused and there is such a generation gap today. But, we survived! What better reason to celebrate?

by Ade Johnson - President Sr. Citizens

Interstate Market Corporation
Chicago, Illinois

Dear Sir:-
Our previous records indicate that you hold stock in the following Companies.
American Can Co.,
Consolidated Gas Co.,
Interstate Water Co.,
Northern Tissue Co.,
Because of uncertain market conditions at this time, it is our recommendation that you sit tight on Your American Can, hold Your Water and let Your Gas Co.

You will be interested to know that today Northern Tissue touched a new bottom and thousands were wiped clean.

Yours truly,

Business Expense Account (with story)

Date	Item	Amt.
4-1	Ad for stenographer	$2.19
4-5	Flowers for new stenographer	4.50
4-9	Weekly salary for stenographer	50.00
4-10	HOSIERY for stenographer	1.75
4-11	Candy for wife	.80
4-12	Lunch with stenographer	5.25
4-13	Weekly salary for stenographer	60.00
4-19	Movie for self and wife	1.20
4-20	Theatre tickets for self & stenographer	9.60
4-21	Coke for wife	.10

5-2	Champagne and dinner for stenographer	32.75
5-3	Dorothy's salary	75.00
5-7	Champagne & dinner with stenographer	41.00
6-28	Doctor	450.00
6-29	Fur coat for wife	975.00
6-30	Ad for male stenographer	2.19

HOW TO BUY YOUR WIFE A MINK

There once was a man who liked to drink and was using all of his family's income at the bars, leaving his wife and kids destitute. So a friend gave him this advice: On Monday morning, go out and buy a fifth of whiskey and give it to your wife. A fifth contains 40 shots. Pay your wife $1.00 a shot and at the end of the week she will have enough money to buy your next fifth plus $32.60 left over. If your wife puts this in the bank on compound interest, at the end of 10 years, she will have $38,464.50. Because of the excessive amount of liquor you drink, you will be dead in 10 years. And your wife will have enough money to bury you, put the kids through college, buy a mink coat, move off of a gol-danged hog farm and marry a decent man that doesn't drink.

A LETTER FROM AN OZARK MOTHER TO HER SON

Dear Son,

I'm writing this real slow cause I know you can't read very fast.

We don't live where we did when you left. Your Daddy read in the paper that most accidents happen within twenty miles of home, so we moved.

I won't be able to send you the address because the last Ozark family that lived here took the numbers off the house with them for their next house so they wouldn't have to change their address.

This place has a washing machine. The first day I put four shirts in, pulled the chain and I ain't seen e'm since.

It only rained twice this week. Three days the first time and four days the second time.

You know the coat you wanted me to send you? Well Aunt Sue said it would be too heavy to send in the mail with them heavy buttons on it, so we cut them off and put them in the pockets.

We got a letter from the funeral home, they said if we don't make the last payment on Grandma's funeral bill, up she comes.

Your sister had a baby this morning. I ain't heard whether it's a boy or girl, so I don't know if you're an uncle or an aunt.

Your Uncle John fell in the whisky vat. Some men tried to pull him out, but he fought them off, so he drowned. We cremated him and he burned for three days.

Three of your friends went off the bridge in a pick-up. One was driving, the other two was in the back. The driver got out. He rolled the window down and swam to safety. The other two drowned. They couldn't get the tailgate down. There's not much news this time, nothing much has happened.

Love,
Mama

From a letter to an
insurance company:

In response to your request for additional information in block number 3 of the accident reporting form, I put "poor Planning" as the cause of my accident. You said in your letter that I should explain more fully, and I trust that the following details will be sufficient.

I am a bricklayer by trade. On the day of the accident, I was working alone on the roof of a new six story building. When I completed my work, I discovered that I had about 500 pounds of brick left over. Rather than carry the bricks down by hand, I decided to lower them in a barrel by using a pulley which fortunately was attached to the side of the building, at the sixth floor.

Securing the rope at ground level, I went up to the roof, swung the barrel out, and loaded the brick into it. Then I went back to the ground and untied the rope, holding it tightly to insure a slow descent of the 500 pounds of bricks. You will note in block number eleven of the accident report form that I weight 135 pounds.

Due to my surprise to being jerked off the ground so suddenly, I lost my presence of mind and forgot to let go of the rope. Needless to say, I proceeded at a rather rapid rate up the side of the building.

In the vicinity of the third floor, I met the barrel coming down. This explains the fractured skull and broken collarbone.

Slowed only slightly, I continued my rapid ascent, not stopping until the fingers of my right hand were two-knuckles deep into the pulley.

Fortunately, by this time I had regained my presence of mind and was able to hold tightly to the rope in spite of my pain.

At approximately the same time, however, the barrel of bricks hit the ground...and the bottom fell out of the barrel. Devoid of the weight of the bricks, the barrel now weighed approximately fifty pounds.

I refer you again to my weight in block number eleven. As you might imagine, I began a rapid descent down the side of the building.

In the vicinity of the third floor, I met the barrel coming up. This accounts for the two fractured ankles and the lacerations of my legs and lower body.

The encounter with the barrel slowed me enough to lessen my injuries when I fell onto the pile of bricks and, fortunately, only three vertebrae were cracked.

I am sorry to report, however, that as I lay there on the bricks – in pain, unable to stand, and watching the empty barrel six stories above me – I again lost my presence of mind....I LET GO OF THE ROPE.

This has been called "The World's Best Collection Letter" because it is most effective – yet achieves results pleasantly.

Dear Mr. _____.

Gosh, all mightly! Oswald (our vice-president has found out about your balance! He is threatening to write to you!

As a friend, I implore you – PAY now, before it is too late! People who get Oswald's collection letters never recover. We hide the Accounts Receivable ledger from, him but he always finds it.

If you could see the results – young men, prematurely aged! Strong men – broken! Usually, Oswald's letters result in 10 percent collections and 90 percent suicides. No one has heard him use any other words than "sue" and "legal action", since the summer of 1902!

Oswald is also President of the Committee for More Death Penalties, and his spare time is spent collecting clippings about hangings!

You see the situation. I like People – particularly customers. I can't stand having them drop off like flies because of Oswald. So please, for your health and my conscience, mail your check NOW for the $ ____ you owe, so you won't get a LETTER FROM OSWALD....may Heaven forbid!

Urgently yours. _____

THE DEER HUNT

1:00 a.m.	Alarm clock rings
2:00 a.m.	Hunting partners arrive, drag you out of bed.
2:15 a.m.	Throw everything except kitchen sink in the pickup
3:00 a.m.	Leave for the deep woods
3:15 a.m.	Drive back home and pick up gun
3:30 a.m.	Drive like hell to get to the woods before daylight
4:00 a.m.	Set up camp – forgot the damn tent
4:30 a.m.	Head into the woods
6:05 a.m.	See 3 deer
6:06 a.m.	Take aim and squeeze trigger
6:07 a.m.	"Click"
6:08 a.m.	Load gun while watching deer go over the hill
8:00 a.m.	Head back to camp
9:00 a.m.	Still looking for camp
10:00 a.m.	Realize you don't know where camp is
NOON	Fire gun for help – eat wild berries
12:15 p.m.	Run out of berries, 3 deer come back
12:20 p.m.	Strange feeling in stomach
12:30 p.m.	Realize you don't know where camp is
12:45 p.m.	Rescued
12:55 p.m.	Rushed to hospital to have stomach pumped
3:00 p.m.	Arrive back in camp
3:30 p.m.	Leave camp to kill deer

4:00 p.m.	Return to camp for bullets
4:01 p.m.	Load gun – leave camp again
5:00 p.m.	Empty gun on squirrel that is bugging you
6:00 p.m.	Arrive at camp, see deer grazing in camp
6:01 p.m.	Load gun
6:02 p.m.	Fire gun
6:03 p.m.	One dead truck
6:05 p.m.	Hunting partner returns to camp dragging deer
6:06 p.m.	Repress strong desire to shoot partner
6:07 p.m.	Fall into fire
6:10 p.m.	Change clothes, throw burned ones in fire
6:15 p.m.	Take pickup and leave partner and his deer in woods
6:25 p.m.	Pickup boils over – hole shot in block
6:26 p.m.	Start Walking
6:30 p.m.	Stumble and fall, drop in mud
6:35 p.m.	Meet bear
6:36 p.m.	Take aim
6:37 p.m.	Fire gun, blows up, barrel plugged with mud
6:38 p.m.	Change my pants
6:39 p.m.	Climb tree
9:00 p.m.	Bear departs, wrap gun around tree
MIDNIGHT	HOME AT LAST
SUNDAY	Watch football game on TV slowly tearing hunting license into

little pieces, place in envelope, and mail to game warden with very clear instructions on where to place it.

 ## The Aging Process

1. Everything hurts-and what doesn't hurt doesn't work.
2. The gleam in your eye is from the sun hitting your bifocals.
3. You feel like the morning after–when you haven't been anywhere.
4. Your "Little Black Book" contains only names ending in "M.D."
5. Your children start to look middle-aged.
6. You get winded playing chess.
7. You know all the answers – but no one asks you the questions.
8. You look forward to a dull evening.
9. You walk with your head held high – trying to get use to your tri-focals.
10. Your favorite part of the paper is "Fifty years ago today."
11. You turn out of the lights for economic reasons – rather than romantic ones.
12. You sit in a rocking chair – but can't get it going.
13. Your knees buckle – and your belt won't.
14. You regret all those mistakes – trying to resist temptation.
15. Dialing Long Distance wears you out.
16. You're 17 around the neck; 42 around the waste; and 96 around the golf course.
17. You're startled when first addressed as an "Old Timer."

BEFORE MARRIAGE

∀ℲTƎꓤ M∀ꓤꓤI∀GE

I quit jogging because it was Bad for my Health

...My thighs rubbed together so much my underwear caught on fire. I get enough exercise being a pallbearer for those who do jog!!¡

WANTED

Woman who can Cook, Dig Worms, Clean Fish, and Owns Boat and Motor

Please send picture of Boat and Motor.

I THINK I'M HAVING STRESS!

I MISS MY MIND

I'm not used to my arthritis,
With my hearing, I'm resigned,
I can manage my bifocals,
But, oh God, I miss my mind!

Sometimes I can't remember
When I stand upon the stairs,
If I'm going up for something
Or I've come down from there.

And often at the Frigidaire
My mind is filled with doubt,
Have I just been putting food away
Or come to take some out?

There are times when in the darkness
with the curlers in my head,
I'm not sure if I'm retiring
Or just getting out of bed.

If it's my time to write you,
There's no need in getting sore,
I might think I've already written
And don't want to be a bore.

Just remember I do miss you
And I wish that you were near
But since it's nearly mail time
I'll say "Au revoir," my dear.

Now I'm standing at the mailbox
With my face completely red,
Instead of mailing you my letter,
I opened it instead!

HILLBILLIES
MEDICAL TERMINOLOGY
FOR THE LAYMEN

ARTERY	The Study of Fine Paintings
BARIUM	What You Do When C.P.R. Fails
CAESAREAN SECTION	A District in Rome
COLIC	A Sheep Dog
CONGENITAL	Friendly
DILATE	To Live Long
FESTER	Quicker
G.I. SERIES	Baseball Games Between Teams of Soldiers
GRIPPE	A Suitcase
HANGNAIL	A Coathook
MEDICAL STAFF	A Doctor's Cane
MINOR OPERATION	Coal Digging
MORBID	A Higher Offer
NITRATE	Lower Than Day Rate
ORGANIC	Church Musician
OUTPATIENT	A Person Who Has Fainted
POST-OPERATIVE	A Letter Carrier
SECRETION	Hiding Anything
SEROLOGY	Study of English Knighthood
TABLET	A Small Table
TUMOR	An Extra Pair
URINE	Opposite Of You're Out
VARICOSE VEINS	Veins Which Are Very Close Together
BENIGN	What You Are After You Be Eight.

DID YOU WANT THE MAN-IN-CHARGE OR THE WOMAN WHO KNOWS WHAT'S GOING ON!

THE MODERN
UNEMPLOYED AMERICAN

This fellow starts out his day early, having set his alarm clock (made in Japan) for 6 a.m. While his coffeepot (made in Japan) is perking, he puts his hair dryer (made in Taiwan) to work and shaves his face with his electric razor (made in Taiwan) He puts on a dress shirt (made in Taiwan) and designer jeans (made in Hong Kong) with a neat pair of tennis shoes (made in Korea). Cuts his grass with a Honda lawnmower (made in Japan). After cooking up some breakfast in his new electric skillet (made in Japan), he sits down to figure out how much he can spend this day on his calculator (made in Mexico). After setting his watch (made in Japan), he goes out, gets in his car (made in Japan), and goes looking for a good paying American Job. At the end of a disgusting day this man decides to relax for a while. He puts on a pair of sandals (made in Brazil), pours himself a glass of wine (made in France) and turns on this TV (made in Japan), all this time trying to figure out why he can't find a good paying American Job!!!

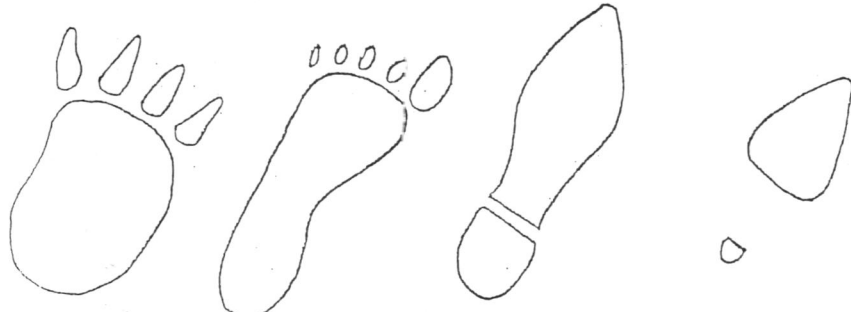

The evolution of authority!

A DAY OFF

So you want the day off. Let's take a look at what you are asking for.........
There are 365 days per year available for work. There are 52 weeks per year in which you already have two days off per week, leaving 261 days available for work. Since you spend 16 hours each day away from work, you have used up 170 days, leaving only 91 days available. You spend 30 minutes each day on coffee break. That accounts for 23 days each year, leaving only 68 days available. With a one hour lunch period each day, you have used up another 46 days, leaving only 22 days available for work. You normally spend 2 days per year on sick leave. This leaves you only 20 days available for work. We are off for five holidays per year, so your available working time is down to 15 days. We generously give you 14 days vacation per year which leaves only 1 day available for work and I'll be damned if you're going to take that day off!!!

Senior Citizens

Are The Biggest Carriers Of

"AIDS"

Hearing Aids, Bandaids,
Rolaids, Walking Aids,
Medicaid, Government Aid,
Etc., Etc.